JOURNAL OF EDUCATIONAL AND PSYCHOLOGICAL CONSULTATION, 11(1), 1–2

Increasing Implementation Success in Prevention Programs

Joseph E. Zins
University of Cincinnati

Maurice J. Elias
Rutgers University

Mark T. Greenberg
Pennsylvania State University

Marsha Kline Pruett
Yale University

This special issue of the *Journal of Educational and Psychological Consultation* represents several years of joint efforts between the Collaborative to Advance Social and Emotional Learning (CASEL) and the Society for Community Research and Action (SCRA) of the American Psychological Association. A call for articles was extended to these organizations, and we are fortunate that a number of their members were able to share their expertise and experiences in program implementation with us through this project. What we believe will be of most importance to readers is that the contributors offer many practical ideas about how to enhance program implementation. Indeed, we learned much from each of them, and we believe you will too.

Important points supporting prevention as an integral aspect of school improvement are made in the first article, by Howard Adelman and Linda Taylor, which is followed by an interesting discussion of a theory of

Correspondence should be addressed to Joseph E. Zins, 339 Teachers College, University of Cincinnati, OH 45221–0002. E-mail: joseph.zins@uc.edu change approach written by James Connell and Adena Klem. Next, Laurie Kramer, Gary Laumann, and Liesette Brunson describe issues related to program diffusion that those working in rural communities face. Full-service schools and integrated service delivery systems have been discussed in the literature in recent years (e.g., Dryfoos, 1994; Illback, Cobb, & Joseph, 1997), but there has been minimal discussion of the problems that may be associated with these initiatives. This topic is the focus of an article by Thomas McMahon, Nadia Ward, Marsha Kline Pruett, Larry Davidson, and Ezra Griffith. In the next article, Geoffrey Nelson, Jeanette Amio, Isaac Prilleltensky, and Peggy Nickels offer some ideas that can guide consultants in implementing programs in partnership with other stakeholders. This special issue concludes with an article in which Charles Diebold, Ginny Miller, Leah Gensheimer, Elaine Mondschein, and Harold Ohmart present a blueprint for planning, implementing, and evaluating prevention programs. The multiple perspectives presented by this diverse group of contributors provide a rich analysis of the field. And, what is also noteworthy, was the risk that was taken by several authors as they described problems they encountered, and discussed mistakes that were made. We thank each of the contributors for their participation and true collegiality in making this special issue possible.

We hope you will enjoy reading this volume as much as we enjoyed organizing and editing it.

REFERENCES

Dryfoos, J. (1994). *Full-service schools: A revolution in health and social services for children, youth, and their families.* San Francisco: Jossey-Bass.

Illback, R. J., Cobb, C., Joseph, H., Jr. (Eds.). (1997). *Integrated services for children and families: Opportunities for psychological practice.* Washington, DC: American Psychological Association.

Journal of Educational and Psychological Consultation

Volume 11, Number 1

JOURNAL OF EDUCATIONAL AND PSYCHOLOGICAL CONSULTATION, 11(1), 3–6

The Role of the Collaborative to Advance Social and Emotional Learning (CASEL) in Supporting the Implementation of Quality School-Based Prevention Programs

Patricia A. Graczyk, Jennifer L. Matjasko, and
Roger P. Weissberg
University of Illinois at Chicago

Mark T. Greenberg
Pennsylvania State University

Maurice J. Elias
Rutgers University

Joseph E. Zins
University of Cincinnati

The Collaborative to Advance Social and Emotional Learning (CASEL) is pleased to have collaborated with the School Intervention Interest Group of the Society for Community Research and Action (SCRA) in the development of this and the next issue of *JEPC*, both of which are devoted to the implementation of effective school-based prevention programs. Founded in 1994, CASEL's mission is to establish social and emotional learning (SEL) as an essential part of a child's education from preschool through high school.

Correspondence should be addressed to Patricia A. Graczyk, Department of Psychology (MC 285), University of Illinois at Chicago, 1007 W. Harrison Street, Chicago, IL 60607–7137.

CASEL has two overarching goals: (a) to advance the science of SEL and (b) to translate scientific findings into effective school-based practices that are used worldwide. To accomplish these goals, CASEL brought together the best thinkers and practitioners in the field of SEL to help schools, families, and communities nurture children's social and emotional development, health-enhancing behaviors, and successful academic performance in school.

SEL can serve as the unifying framework under which schools can organize various competence-building and preventive efforts (e.g., problem solving, conflict resolution, drug abuse prevention) because of SEL's dual focus on building student competencies and establishing supportive environmental settings (Elias et al., 1997). Specifically, social and emotional education programs enhance the capacities of students to coordinate emotion, cognition, and behavior so they can effectively and ethically handle developmentally relevant tasks. In addition, SEL programs establish environmental settings and resources that encourage students to become knowledgeable, responsible, and caring individuals who can achieve positive academic, health, and citizenship outcomes. However, the effectiveness of even well-designed and empirically validated programs in promoting positive youth development can be attenuated if they are implemented in ways that compromise their integrity.

One of CASEL's major initiatives is to identify and promote practices that insure the effective implementation of school-based competence-building and prevention efforts. To further the scientific foundation for successful implementation practices, CASEL cosponsored an invitational conference on implementation research at Penn State University in October 1999. This meeting was convened by Mark Greenberg and Joseph Zins and was attended by 20 prominent prevention researchers and federal officials. Participants discussed issues relative to the study and assessment of implementation processes. In addition, they identified critical factors that may contribute to a school's ability to provide high quality SEL and prevention programs that lead to positive outcomes for children and youth. The conference was successful in launching several important follow-up projects, including (a) a multi-site collaborative effort to study the implementation process, (b) the compilation of measures currently being used to assess implementation quality, and (c) a series of papers targeting a variety of audiences in which the current state of the science and the practice of implementation is described and specific recommendations are made to advance the field. In addition to its efforts toward insuring successful implementation of school-based programs, CASEL has four other major initiatives currently underway that may be of interest to *JEPC* readers:

1. *SEL Program Review:* The focus of CASEL's SEL Program Review is to identify key elements of SEL and determine the degree to which available school-based programs include these elements. Findings of the review will be published in a consumers' guide for educators to help them select exemplary programs and will be used to inform the field about ways to improve future programmatic efforts.

2. *SEL and Educational Outcomes:* This project will synthesize the scientific literature linking SEL to broadly defined measures of school success such as academic performance, school attendance, and participation in school activities. The findings will be shared with researchers, educational leaders, and policy makers through publications and invitational conferences.

3. *SEL and Health Outcomes:* CASEL is collaborating with the Center for the Advancement of Health in synthesizing the scientific literature connecting social and emotional competence in children to various health outcomes. This project will culminate in a monograph of the findings and an indexed bibliography to be widely distributed and promoted to relevant audiences.

4. *Educator Preparation and Practice:* CASEL has facilitated interactions among leading SEL program developers and implementers enabling them to share strategies to prepare educators to implement quality SEL programs. This group is developing content and materials for SEL courses that will be offered in several colleges of education as well as for in-service training for practicing educators.

Information on all these projects is posted and regularly updated on CASEL's web site (www.casel.org). Readers of *JEPC* are encouraged to visit our web site and communicate with us via e-mail (casel@uic.edu) to keep abreast of CASEL and the field of social and emotional learning.

ACKNOWLEDGMENTS

The authors wish to acknowledge support for CASEL provided by the United States Department of Education, the Surdna Foundation, the Joseph P. Kennedy, Jr. Foundation, and the Fetzer Institute. The work of the first author has been supported, in part, by a post-doctoral fellowship from the

National Institute of Mental Health in Urban Children's Mental Health and HIV/AIDS Prevention (#1–T32–MH19933).

REFERENCE

Elias, M. J., Zins, J. E., Weissberg, R. P., Frey, K. S., Greenberg, M. T., Haynes, N. M., Kessler, R., Schwab-Stone, M. E., & Shriver, T. P. (1997). *Promoting social and emotional learning: Guidelines for educators.* Alexandria, VA: Association for Supervision and Curriculum Development.

Patricia A. Graczyk is CASEL's Senior Research Associate and a post-doctoral fellow in the National Institutes of Mental Health Prevention Research Training Program at the University of Illinois at Chicago.

Jennifer L. Matjasko is CASEL's Director of Communications and Networking, and a doctoral candidate in public policy at the University of Chicago.

Roger P. Weissberg is CASEL's Executive Director and Professor of Psychology and Education at the University of Illinois at Chicago.

Mark T. Greenberg is a member of CASEL's Leadership Team and Director of the Prevention Research Center at Pennsylvania State University.

Maurice J. Elias is a member of CASEL's Leadership Team and Professor of Psychology at Rutgers University.

Joseph E. Zins is a member of CASEL's Leadership Team and a professor at the University of Cincinnati.

JOURNAL OF EDUCATIONAL AND PSYCHOLOGICAL CONSULTATION, 11(1), 7–36

Moving Prevention From the Fringes Into the Fabric of School Improvement

Howard S. Adelman

University of California, Los Angeles

Linda Taylor

Los Angeles Unified School District and
University of California, Los Angeles

If prevention initiatives are to get beyond their current marginalized and fragmented status, they must be framed in a comprehensive context. This article places primary prevention at one end of a comprehensive continuum of interventions and explores the continuum in terms of a component for addressing barriers to development and learning. Such a component is conceptualized as primary and essential to successful school reform. Current concerns and emerging trends related to policy, research, practice, and training are highlighted, and general implications for systemic changes are suggested.

The term prevention conjures up a variety of reactions. Few would argue against the desirability of preventing educational and psychological problems. However, some leaders in the field have lamented that prevention initiatives are still too oriented to risk reduction, which often works against efforts to promote wellness as an invaluable mental health end in and of itself (e.g., Cowen, 1997). In schools, the orientation to reducing risk has led to an overemphasis on observed problems and on treating them as discrete entities. This contributes to de-emphasizing common underlying causes and their treatment. Such a state of affairs is both a result and an ongoing

---

Correspondence should be addressed to Howard S. Adelman, Department of Psychology, UCLA, Box 951563, Los Angeles, CA 90095–1563. E-mail: adelman@psych.ucla.edu

factor in perpetuating widespread fragmentation of prevention initiatives at all levels. A vicious cycle of unsatisfactory policy and practice has emerged. And, the cycle is likely to continue as long as policy priorities for prevention are so low that the enterprise remains a marginalized aspect of systemic reforms. These concerns are of major relevance to anyone interested in preventing problems on a large scale.

If prevention initiatives are to get beyond their current marginalized and fragmented status, they must be framed in a comprehensive context. With this in mind, we begin with a presentation that places primary prevention at one end of a comprehensive continuum of interventions. Then, the continuum is explored in terms of a component for addressing barriers to development and learning that is viewed as primary and essential to successful school reform. Throughout the article, implications are discussed with respect to policy, research, practice, and training.

FRAMING PREVENTION AS ONE END OF A COMPREHENSIVE, MULTIFACETED CONTINUUM OF INTERVENTION

Prevention initiatives have many facets. At a school, approaches may be school wide with the intent of having an impact on all students; they may be limited to a classroom; they may target a specific group and a specific problem. Various strategies may be used to promote healthy development or address factors that interfere with positive functioning. Table 1 outlines some key categories that can aid in differentiating among school-oriented prevention efforts. As outlined, the term *prevention* encompasses discrete strategies and broad, multifaceted approaches.

Policy-oriented discussions increasingly recognize the importance of multifaceted approaches to account for social, economic, political, and cultural factors that can interfere with or promote development, learning, and teaching (Center for Mental Health in Schools, 1996, 1997; Dryfoos, 1998; Schorr, 1997). For purposes of analyzing the state of the art and making recommendations, major policies and practices for addressing such factors can be grouped into five areas. The areas are:

1. Measures to abate inequities or restricted opportunities.
2. Primary prevention and early age interventions.
3. Identification and amelioration of learning, behavior, emotional, and health problems as early as is feasible.
4. Ongoing amelioration of mild to moderate learning, behavior, emotional, and health problems.

TABLE 1

Outline Aid for Analyzing Key Facets of School-Oriented Prevention Efforts

I. **Form of initiative.**
   A. Policy (federal, state, local).
   B. Practice.
   C. Capacity building.
   D. Systemic change.

II. **Context for practice.**
   A. Community wide.
   B. School wide.
   C. In classroom as part of regular program.
   D. An "add-on" program in or outside the regular class.
   E. Part of "clinical" services.

III. **Stage of prevention.**
   A. Primary.
   B. Secondary.
   C. Tertiary.

IV. **Focus.**
   A. Focal point of intervention.
      1. Environment(s).
      2. Person(s).
      3. Both.
   B. Intended range of impact.
      1. A broad-band intervention.
      2. For one or more specific targets.
   C. Breadth of approach.
      1. Directed at a categorical problem.
      2. Multifaceted.
   D. General area of concern.
      1. Addressing barriers to development, learning, and positive functioning.
      2. Promoting healthy development.
   E. Domain.
      1. Knowledge.
      2. Skills.
      3. Attitudes.
   F. Strategy.
      1. Instruction.[a]
      2. Behavior modification.
      3. Enhancing expectations and opportunities for positive behavior.

   4. Counseling/therapy.
   5. Physical health programs and services.
   6. Social support.
   7. Social services.
   8. Student to student support and socialization.
   9. School–home–community partnerships.
   10. Enhancing security and policing measures.
   11. Multiple strategies.
   12. Comprehensive, school-wide approaches.

V. **Level of schooling/student development.**
   A. Elementary/middle/high school.
   B. Specific grade, age, or stage of development.

VI. **Degree of integration with other interventions.**
   A. Isolated.
   B. Coordinated with others.
   C. Systematically integrated.

VII. **Stage of intervention development.**
   A. Formative.
   B. Fully developed, but unevaluated.
   C. Empirically supported.

VIII. **Scope of implementation.**
   A. Limited project.
      1. At one site.
      2. At several sites.
   B. Systemic change initiative.
      1. Still at pilot demonstration stage.
      2. Being phased in—at a few sites.
      3. Being phased in—at many sites.
      4. All sites involved.

IX. **Approach to evaluation.**
   A. Focused only on accountability demands.
   B. Formative program evaluation.
   C. Summative program evaluation.
      1. Of efficacy.
      2. Of effectiveness when replicated under natural conditions.
      3. Cost-effectiveness analyses.
   D. Designed as evaluation research.

Note. When the emphasis is on curriculum to prevent psychosocial problems (violence, substance abuse, delinquency, pregnancy, eating disorders, learning problems, etc.) and/or promote healthy socioemotional development and effective functioning, the *content focus* may be on

(Continued)

TABLE 1 *(Continued)*

- Assets-building (including strengthening academics, developing protective factors, expanding areas of competence and self-discipline).
- Socioemotional development (e.g., understanding self and others, enhancing positive feelings toward self and others, cognitive and interpersonal problemsolving, social skills, emotional "intelligence").
- Building character (e.g., values).
- Physical development (e.g., diet/nutrition, sports/recreation).
- Fostering abilities (e.g., one or more of the multiple "intelligences," enrichment).
- Fostering hope (e.g., positive expectations for the future; perceptions of self-determination).
- Resistance education.
- Stress reduction.
- Symptom reduction.

[a]Content focus of curricular approaches.

5. Ongoing treatment of and support for chronic or severe or pervasive problems.

As illustrated in Figure 1, the range of interventions can be further appreciated by viewing them on a continuum ranging from primary prevention (including a focus on wellness or competence enhancement), through approaches for treating problems early-after-onset, and extending on to narrowly focused treatments for severe or chronic problems.[1] Such a continuum provides a template for assessing the degree to which the package of community and school programs serving local geographic or catchment areas is comprehensive, multifaceted, and integrated. It encompasses the concepts of primary, secondary, and tertiary prevention. It is intended to incorporate a holistic and developmental emphasis that envelops individuals, families, and the contexts in which they live, work, and play. The examples offered in Figure 1 reflect a basic assumption that many problems are not discrete, and therefore, interventions that address root causes can minimize the trend to develop separate programs for every observed problem. Another assumption is that the least restrictive and nonintrusive forms of intervention required to appropriately address problems and accommodate diversity should be used.

The range of programs cited in Figure 1 are seen as integrally related, and it seems likely that the impact of each can be exponentially increased through coordination and integration. Such connections may involve hori-

---

[1]There are too many references to cite here, but a bit of an overview of work that is directly relevant to school-based and linked interventions can be garnered from Adelman and Taylor (1993), Albee and Gullotta (1997), Borders and Drury (1992), Carnegie Council on Adolescent Development (1988), Dryfoos (1990, 1994, 1998), Durlak (1995), Duttweiler (1995), Goleman (1995), Henggeler (1995), Hoagwood and Erwin (1997), Karoly et al. (1998), Kazdin (1993), Larson (1994), Scattergood, Dash, Epstein, and Adler (1998), Schorr (1988, 1997), Slavin, Karweit, & Wasik (1994), and Thomas and Grimes (1995).

Intervention Continuum	Examples of Focus and Types of Intervention (Programs and services aimed at system changes and individual needs)
Primary prevention	1. *Public health protection, promotion, and maintenance to foster opportunities, positive development, and wellness* • economic enhancement of those living in poverty • safety • physical and mental health
	2. *Support and assistance to enhance health and psychosocial development for preschoolers and during early schooling* • systems' enhancement through capacity building and cross-disciplinary collegial teaming and assistance • education and social support for parents and surrogates • quality day care/quality early education • personalized instruction • preparation and support for school and life transitions • enhanced curricular and extra-curricular enrichment and recreation programs • increased opportunities for young people to assume positive roles
Early-after-onset intervention	• appropriate screening and amelioration of physical and mental health and psychosocial problems • support and guidance to ameliorate school adjustment problems • additional support to address specific learning problems • enhanced home involvement in problem solving • comprehensive and accessible psychosocial and physical and mental health programs
	3. *Improvement and augmentation of ongoing regular support* • enhance systems via school-wide approaches and school-community partnerships to build capacity and enhance cross-disciplinary collegial teaming and assistance • teaching "basics" of support and remediation to regular teachers • resource support for parents-in-need • comprehensive and accessible psychosocial and physical and mental health interventions • Academic guidance and assistance • Emergency and crisis prevention and response mechanisms
	4. *Other interventions prior to referral for intensive, ongoing treatments* • enhance systems via school-wide approaches and school-community partnerships to build capacity and enhance cross-disciplinary collegial teaming and assistance • short-term specialized interventions
Treatment for severe/chronic problems	5. *Intensive treatments* • referral, triage, placement guidance and assistance, management of care, and resource coordination • family preservation programs and services • special education, rehabilitation, and alternative placements • dropout recovery and follow-up support • services for severe-chronic psychosocial/mental/physical health problems • systems of care

FIGURE 1   From primary prevention to treatment of serious problems: A continuum of community-school programs. From *Learning problems and learning disabilites: Moving forward* (p. 279) by H. S. Adelman & L. Taylor, 1993, Pacific Grove, CA: Brooks/Cole. Copyright 1993 by Wadsworth Publishing, a division of Thomson Learning. Fax: (800)730–2215. Adapted with permission.

zontal and vertical restructuring of programs and services (a) within jurisdictions, school districts, and community agencies (e.g., among
departments, divisions, units) and (b) between jurisdictions, school and
community agencies, public and private sectors, among clusters of
schools, and among community agencies. Ultimately, such a continuum
should be developed into systems of prevention, systems of early intervention, and systems of care (see Figure 2). And each of these systems must be
connected effectively.

Unfortunately, implementation of a full continuum of programs with
an extensive range of activities does not occur in communities that must
rely on underwriting from public funds and private philanthropic organi-

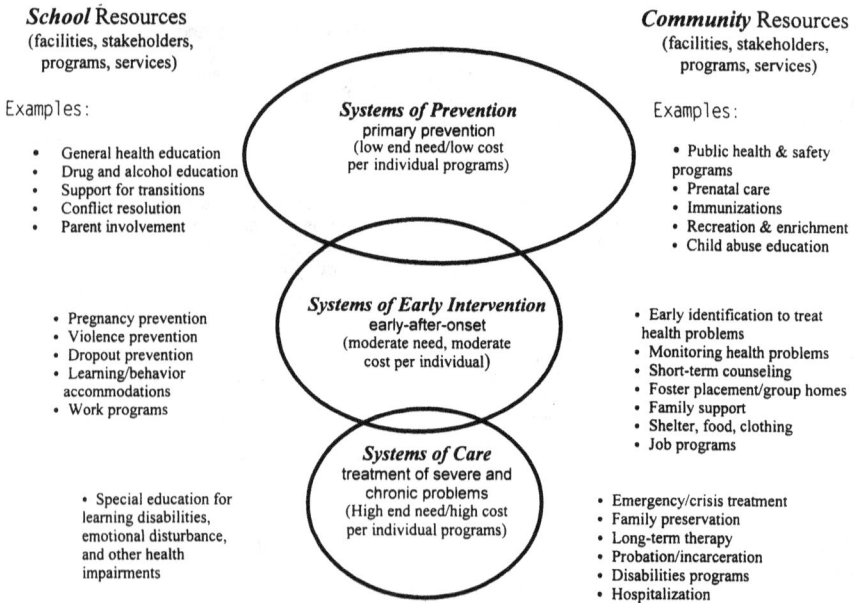

School Resources
(facilities, stakeholders,
programs, services)

Community Resources
(facilities, stakeholders,
programs, services)

Examples:

- General health education
- Drug and alcohol education
- Support for transitions
- Conflict resolution
- Parent involvement

Systems of Prevention
primary prevention
(low end need/low cost
per individual programs)

Examples:

- Public health & safety
  programs
- Prenatal care
- Immunizations
- Recreation & enrichment
- Child abuse education

- Pregnancy prevention
- Violence prevention
- Dropout prevention
- Learning/behavior
  accommodations
- Work programs

Systems of Early Intervention
early-after-onset
(moderate need, moderate
cost per individual)

- Early identification to treat
  health problems
- Monitoring health problems
- Short-term counseling
- Foster placement/group homes
- Family support
- Shelter, food, clothing
- Job programs

- Special education for
  learning disabilities,
  emotional disturbance,
  and other health
  impairments

Systems of Care
treatment of severe and
chronic problems
(High end need/high cost
per individual programs)

- Emergency/crisis treatment
- Family preservation
- Long-term therapy
- Probation/incarceration
- Disabilities programs
- Hospitalization

FIGURE 2   Interconnected systems for meeting the needs of all students. Systemic collaboration* is essential to establish interprogram connections on a daily basis and over time to ensure seamless intervention within each system and among *systems of prevention, systems of early intervention,* and *systems of care.*

*Such colaboration involves horizontal and vertical restructuring of programs and services
    (a) within jurisdictions, school districts, and community agencies (e.g., among departments,
    divisons, units, schools, clusters of schools).
    (b) between jurisdictions, school and community agencies, public and private sectors; among
    schools; among community agencies.

zations. It is painfully clear that few schools do more than give short shrift to efforts that prevent and ameliorate barriers to development and learning. In particular, prevention programs are few in number and usually are funded as discrete projects often with "soft" money (e.g., see projects described in Bond & Compas, 1989; Cowen & Hightower, 1996; Durlak, 1995; Scattergood et al., 1998). Moreover, what programs are in place are fragmented. And this means there is not the type of systemic collaboration that is essential for establishing interprogram connections on a daily basis and over time.

FRAMING POLICY IN TERMS OF ADDRESSING BARRIERS TO DEVELOPMENT AND LEARNING

It is one thing to stress the desirability of framing primary prevention as one end of a continuum of intervention; it is quite another to argue that schools should pursue the type of comprehensive approach outlined above. The success of such an argument probably depends on framing it in the context of the mission of schools and with reference to current initiatives for school reform. That is, it must be rooted in the reality that schools are first and foremost accountable for educating the young. It must appreciate that what interest schools have shown in addressing designated problems mostly reflects a long-held understanding that certain problems are barriers to student learning. Some of these stem from primary internal problems or disabilities that lead to learning, behavior, and emotional dysfunction. Fortunately, relatively few youngsters start out with such problems. For many children and adolescents, however, it is patently evident that a range of external factors that interfere with schools accomplishing their mission are at play. Anyone who works with young people is all too familiar with the litany of such factors (e.g., violence, drugs, frequent school changes, and a host of problems that confront recent immigrants and families living in poverty). It is this state of affairs that argues for schools and communities offering much more in the way of prevention programs.

Prevailing Policy Trends

From our perspective, the policies shaping current agendas for school reform and community agency restructuring are seriously flawed. In recent years, policymakers have stressed the relation between limited intervention efficacy and the widespread tendency for complementary programs to operate in isolation. Limited efficacy does seem inevitable as long as interventions are carried out in a piecemeal fashion and with little follow through. Therefore, reformers have directed restructuring activity toward reducing service fragmentation and increasing access to health and social services. Although these are significant concerns, they are not the most basic ones, and it is unlikely that even these concerns can be resolved appropriately in the absence of concerted attention in policy and practice to ending the marginalized status of efforts to address factors interfering with development, learning, and teaching.

   Policies focused on integrated services and school-linked services are insufficient.   The call for integrated services clearly is motivated by a desire to reduce redundancy, waste, and ineffectiveness resulting from fragmentation (Adler & Gardner, 1994). Special attention is given to the many piecemeal, categorically funded approaches, such as those created to reduce learning and behavior problems, substance abuse, violence, school dropouts, delinquency, teen pregnancy, and so forth. And, ironically, initiatives to colocate community services on school sites can increase fragmentation.
   By focusing primarily on the aforementioned matters, policy makers fail to deal with the overriding issue, namely that addressing barriers to development and learning remains a marginalized aspect of policy and practice. As long as this is the case, reforms to reduce fragmentation and to increase access are seriously hampered. More to the point, the desired impact for large numbers of children and adolescents will not be achieved.

   Community strategies to enhance youth development also are insufficient.   Some initiatives for school-linked services have meshed with the emerging movement to expand school and community strategies and to enhance the infrastructure for youth development (Burt, 1998; Cahill, 1994, 1998; Catalano & Hawkins, 1995; Dryfoos, 1998; Schorr, 1997). Currently, the growing youth development movement encompasses a range of concepts and practices aimed at promoting protective factors, asset-building, wellness, and empowerment. Youth development initiatives clearly expand intervention beyond services and programs. However, they still represent a marginalized set of strategies, and thus the movement's success also seems unlikely, unless its status in the public policy arena is enhanced considerably.

Toward Countering Marginalization

For prevention to play a significant role in the lives of children and their families, policy and practice must undergo a radical transformation. Because the focus on addressing barriers is so marginalized, schools and communities continue to operate with virtually no comprehensive frameworks to guide their thinking about the most *potent* approaches to widespread prevention. The consequences of all this are seen in the lack of attention given these matters in consolidated plans and program quality reviews and the lack of efforts to map, analyze, and rethink resource allocation; the impact is also apparent in the token way these concerns are dealt with in designing preservice and continuing education agendas for administrative and line staff; and on and on.

Policy must foster a full continuum of integrated systems.   A major breakthrough in the battle against learning, behavior, and emotional problems probably can be achieved only when a full range of programs are implemented. Developing comprehensive approaches requires more than specific prevention and early intervention programs, more than outreach to link with community resources (and certainly more than adopting a school-linked services model), more than coordinating school-owned services, more than coordinating school services with community services, and more than creating Family Resource Centers, Full Service Schools, and Community Schools. None of these constitute school- or community-wide approaches, and the growing consensus is that comprehensive, multifaceted, and integrated approaches are essential in addressing the complex concerns confronting schools, families, and neighborhoods (e.g., Adelman, 1993, 1996a, 1996b; Adelman & Taylor, 1997; Catalano & Hawkins, 1995; Comer, 1997; Dryfoos, 1998; Greenwald, Hedges, & Laine, 1996; Sailor & Skrtic, 1996; Schorr, 1997).

Unfortunately, when it comes to addressing barriers, there are too few guidelines delineating basic areas around which to develop a broad-based continuum of interventions. The frameworks illustrated in Figures 1 and 2 provide a beginning. From our perspective, a high level of policy emphasis on developing a comprehensive, multifaceted continuum is the key not only to unifying fragmented activity, but also to using all available resources in the most productive manner.

Expanding school reform.   Because no comprehensive approach can be established without weaving together school and community resources, it is essential to develop models and policies that expand the nature and scope of school reform. Indeed, it is time for a basic policy shift. In this regard, we have proposed that policy makers move from the inadequate, two-component model that dominates school reform to a three-component framework (see Adelman, 1996a, 1996b; Adelman & Taylor, 1994, 1997, 1998; Center for Mental Health in Schools, 1996, 1997, 1998). The continued failure of current models for school reform suggests that better achievement surely requires more than good instruction and well-managed schools (Tyack & Cuban, 1995).

As highlighted in Figures 3 and 4, a three component model calls for elevating efforts to address barriers to learning, development, and teaching to a high level of policy focus. That is, a component that comprehensively enables learning by addressing barriers is seen as a fundamental and essential facet of educational reform. When policy and practice are viewed through the lens of this third component, it becomes evident

How does current policy, practice, and research address barriers to student learning?

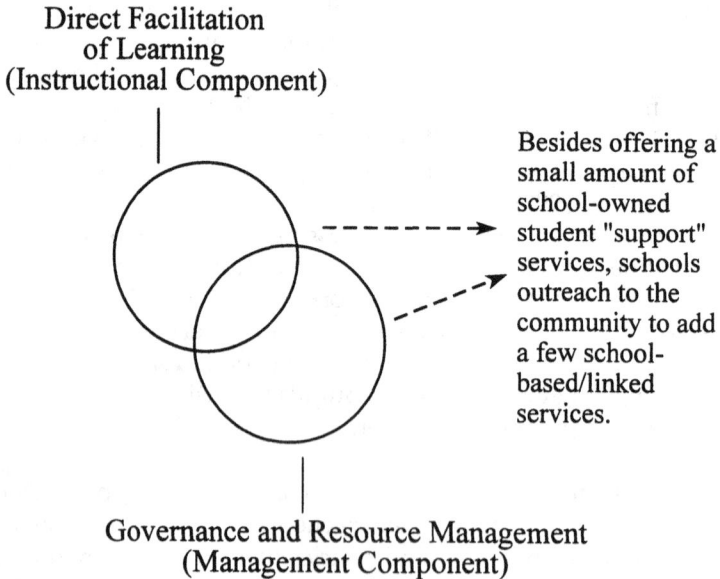

Direct Facilitation
of Learning
(Instructional Component)

Besides offering a small amount of school-owned student "support" services, schools outreach to the community to add a few school-based/linked services.

Governance and Resource Management
(Management Component)

FIGURE 3   A two component model for reform and restructuring.

*What type of policy, practice, and research are needed
to address barriers to learning more effectively?*

Direct Facilitation
of Learning
(Instructional Component)

Addressing Barriers
to Learning
(Enabling Component*)

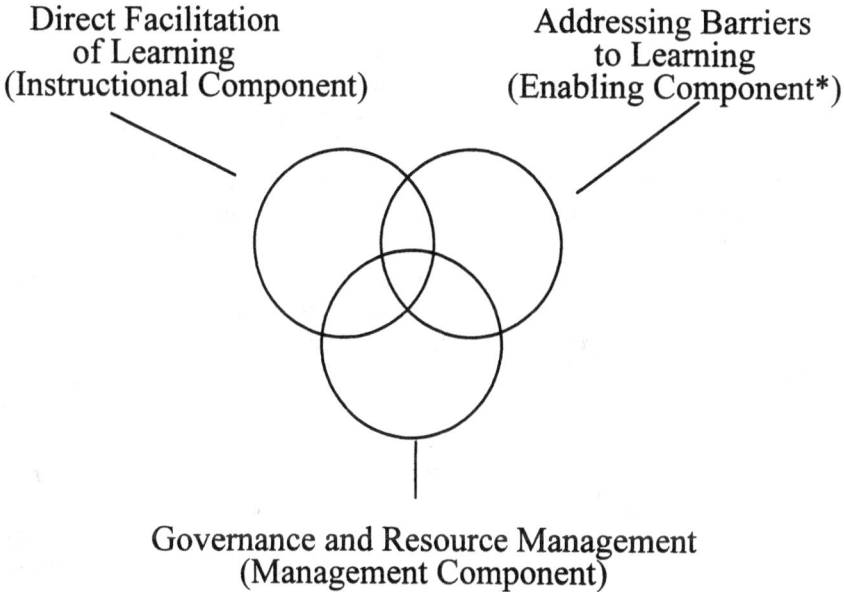

Governance and Resource Management
(Management Component)

FIGURE 4   A three component model for reform and restructuring.

* A component which is treated as primary and essential and which weaves together
school and community resources to devlop comprehensive, multifaceted approaches
to addressing barriers.

how much is missing in current efforts to enable all students to learn and
develop.

The concept of an enabling component was formulated to encompass a
third component (Adelman, 1996a, 1996b; Adelman & Taylor, 1994, 1997,
1998). It provides a basis for combating marginalization and a focal point
for developing a comprehensive framework for policy and practice. It can
also help address fragmentation by providing a unifying term for dispa-
rate approaches to preventing and to ameliorating psychosocial problems
and to promoting wellness. The usefulness of the concept of an enabling
component as a broad, unifying focal point for policy and practice is evi-
denced in its adoption by the California Department of Education (whose

version is called *Learning Supports*) and by one of the New American School's design teams (Urban Learning Center, 1995). It is also attracting attention in various states and localities around the country.

Emergence of a cohesive enabling component requires policy reform and operational restructuring that allow for the weaving together of what is available at a school; expanding this through integrating school, community, and home resources; and enhancing access to community resources by linking as many as is feasible to programs at the school. This involves extensive restructuring of school-owned enabling activity, such as pupil services and special and compensatory education programs, and doing so in ways that fully integrate the enabling, instructional, and management components. In the process, mechanisms must be developed to coordinate and to eventually integrate school-owned enabling activity with community-owned resources (e.g., formally connecting school programs with assets at home, in the business and faith communities, and neighborhood enrichment, recreation, and service resources).

It is important to stress that addressing barriers is not a separate agenda from a school's instructional mission. In policy, practice, and research, all categorical programs can be integrated into a comprehensive component for addressing barriers. Analyses indicate that schools can build an enabling component by developing programs in six basic areas (see Figure 5 and the Appendix). Work carried out in the context of school reform indicates that delineating these six areas for schools can foster comprehensive, multifaceted approaches that encompass school–community partnerships (Adelman, 1996b; Adelman & Taylor, 1994; Urban Learning Center, 1995).

NEEDED: SYSTEMIC RESTRUCTURING AND PERSONNEL RETRAINING AT ALL LEVELS

The type of policy and practice changes outlined previously carry with them calls for restructuring systemic mechanisms and personnel roles and functions at schools, central offices, and school boards. With respect to preventing and ameliorating problems, well-redesigned organizational and operational mechanisms can provide the means for schools to (a) arrive at wise decisions about resource allocation; (b) maximize systematic and integrated planning, implementation, maintenance, and evaluation of enabling activity; (c) outreach to create formal working relationships with community resources to bring some to a school and establish special linkages with others; and (d) upgrade and modernize interventions to reflect the best models and use of technology. Implied in all this are new roles and

Range of Learners
(categorized in terms of their
 response to academic instruction)

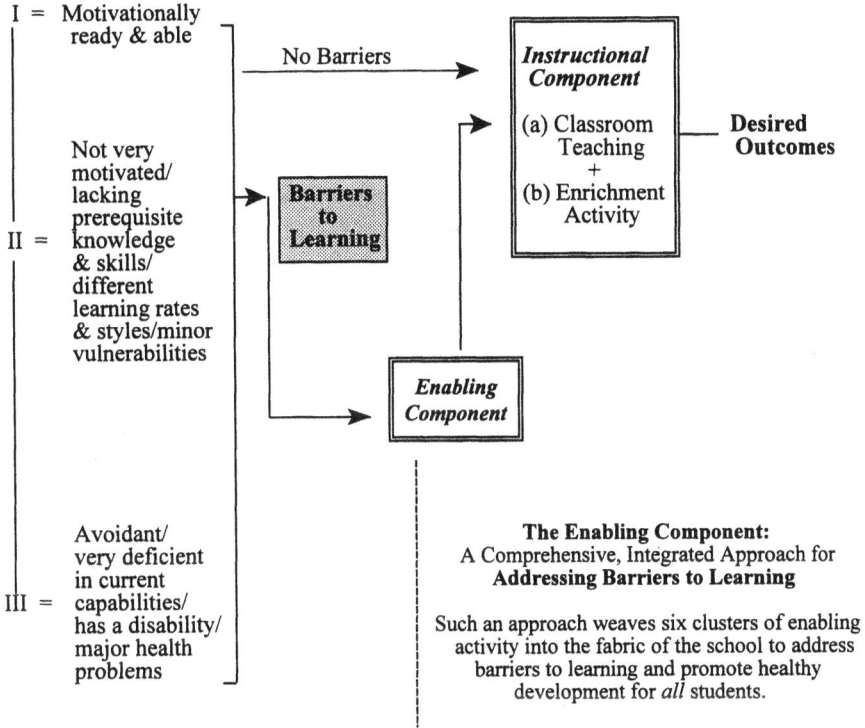

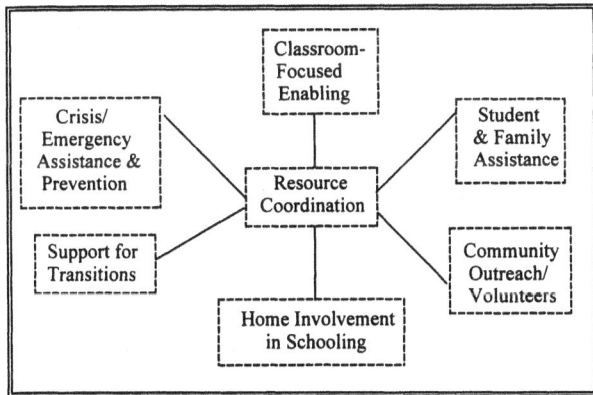

I = Motivationally
    ready & able

No Barriers → ***Instructional Component***

(a) Classroom
    Teaching
    +
(b) Enrichment
    Activity

Desired Outcomes

II = Not very
     motivated/
     lacking
     prerequisite
     knowledge
     & skills/
     different
     learning rates
     & styles/minor
     vulnerabilities

Barriers to Learning

Enabling Component

III = Avoidant/
      very deficient
      in current
      capabilities/
      has a disability/
      major health
      problems

The Enabling Component:
A Comprehensive, Integrated Approach for
Addressing Barriers to Learning

Such an approach weaves six clusters of enabling
activity into the fabric of the school to address
barriers to learning and promote healthy
development for *all* students.

Classroom-
Focused
Enabling

Crisis/
Emergency
Assistance &
Prevention

Student
& Family
Assistance

Support for
Transitions

Resource
Coordination

Community
Outreach/
Volunteers

Home Involvement
in Schooling

FIGURE 5   An enabling component to address barriers to learning and enhance healthy development at a school site.

19

functions for some staff and greater involvement of parents, students, and other representatives from the community. Also implied is redeployment of existing resources as well as finding new ones.

New Mechanisms

From a decentralized perspective, the focus is first on systemic changes at the school level. Then, based on analyses of what is needed to facilitate and enhance school level efforts, changes are conceived for families of schools. Finally, appropriate central office restructuring can be pursued, with clarity about what is needed to facilitate school-based models. Awareness of the myriad political and bureaucratic difficulties involved in making major institutional changes, especially with limited financial resources, leads to the caution that such large-scale restructuring is not likely to proceed in straight-forward, sequential steps. Experience indicates the changes emerge in overlapping and spiraling phases. Offered next are a few examples of systemic changes we are fostering with the intent of moving school reform from a two- to a three-component model (again, see Figures 3 and 4).

Resource-oriented teams at schools, complexes, and system wide.   Currently, many schools do not have mechanisms focused specifically on how to prevent and ameliorate barriers to learning and teaching. No administrator or team has responsibility for mapping existing efforts, analyzing how well resources are being used to meet needs, and planning how to enhance such efforts. An example of mechanisms designed for these purposes can be seen in work related to building into the structure of every school a resource coordinating team, creating a resource coordinating council for a complex, or "family," of schools, and creating a system-wide steering body (Adelman, 1993; Adelman & Taylor, 1993, 1998; Lim & Adelman, 1997; Rosenblum, DiCecco, Taylor, & Adelman, 1995).

A resource-oriented team differs from those created to review students (e.g., a student study or success team, a teacher-assistance team, a case management team). That is, its focus is not on specific cases, but on clarifying resources and their best use. Such a team provides what often is a missing mechanism for managing and enhancing *systems* to coordinate, integrate, and strengthen interventions. For example, at a school site, a resource coordinating team can be assigned responsibility for (a) identifying and analyzing activity and resources with a view to improving the school's efforts to prevent and ameliorate problems; (b) ensuring there are effective systems for prereferral interventions, referral, case management, and quality assurance; (c) guaranteeing appropriate procedures for effective management of programs and for communication among school staff and with the home; and (d) exploring ways to redeploy and enhance resources, such as clarifying which activities are nonproductive and suggesting better uses for the resources, as well as reaching out to connect with additional resources in the school district and community.

Creation of resource-oriented teams provides essential mechanisms for starting to weave together existing school and community resources and encourage services and programs to function in an increasingly cohesive way. Such teams are also vehicles for building working relationships and can play a role in solving turf and operational problems; developing plans to ensure availability of a coordinated set of efforts; and generally improving the attention paid to developing a comprehensive, integrated approach for addressing barriers to student learning.

1. Mapping, analyzing, and enhancing resources. In schools and community agencies, there is redundancy stemming from ill-conceived policies and lack of coordination. These facts do not translate into evidence that there are pools of unneeded personnel and programs; they simply suggest there are resources that can be used in different ways to address unmet needs. Given that additional funding for reform is hard to come by, such redeployment of resources is the primary answer to the ubiquitous question, where will we find the funds?

Thus, one of the primary and essential tasks a resource-oriented team undertakes is that of enumerating school and community programs and services that are in place to support students, families, and staff. A comprehensive form of "needs assessment" is generated as resource mapping is paired with surveys of the unmet needs of students, their families, and school staff. Analyses of what is available, effective, and needed, provides a sound basis for formulating strategies to link with additional resources at other schools, district sites, and in the community and to enhance use of existing resources. Such analyses can also guide efforts to improve cost-effectiveness. In a similar fashion, a resource-oriented team for a complex, or family, of schools (e.g., a high school and its feeders) provides a mechanism for analyses that can lead to strategies for cooperation and integration to enhance intervention effectiveness and to garner economies of scale.

2. An enhanced role in program development and governance. Where creation of "another team" is seen as a burden, existing teams can be asked to broaden their scope. At school sites, teams, such as student study or success teams, teacher assistance teams, site-based management teams, and school crisis teams, have extended their functions to encompass resource mapping, analyses, coordination, and enhancement. To do so, however, they must take great care to structure their agenda so that sufficient time is devoted to the additional tasks.

Although a resource-oriented team might be created solely around psychosocial programs, such a mechanism is meant to bring together representatives of all major programs and services that support the instructional component (e.g., guidance counselors, school psychologists, nurses, social workers, attendance and dropout counselors, health educators, special education staff, after school program staff, bilingual and Title I program coordinators, health educators, safe and drug-free school staff). This also includes representatives of any community agency that is significantly involved with schools. Beyond these service providers, such a team is well-advised to add the energies and expertise of administrators, regular classroom teachers, noncertificated staff, parents, and older students.

School-site and central office leadership. School and multisite resource-oriented teams are not sufficient. Site and system-wide policy guidance, leadership, and assistance are required. For example, it is unlikely that a school can create, institutionalize, and foster ongoing renewal of a comprehensive approach to addressing barriers to learning without an administrator who has the time and competence to lead the way. Thus, one clear implication of a policy shift that embraces a component to address barriers to learning is to restructure administrative roles and functions. At many schools, this would involve the assignment of an assistant principal who can devote at least 50% of his or her time to oversight and development of an enabling component. The functions of this role include vision building and strategic planning for creating the component; facilitating ongoing program planning, implementation, and evaluation; and ensuring its integration with the instructional and management components. In most cases, the assigned administrator will require a fair amount of on-the-job training to carry out these functions effectively. Once the new policies take hold on a large scale, relevant changes can be expected in administrative credentialing programs.

At the central office level, leadership must focus on supporting school and cluster level activity. That is, such leadership must ensure that system-wide resources are truly designed to support the work of school-sites in the most effective and efficient ways. This role requires much more than distributing a "fair" share to everyone. It encompasses capacity building strategies that facilitate school-site development of comprehensive approaches for preventing and ameliorating problems, including creating readiness for systemic change, leadership training, stakeholder development, and capitalizing on commonalities across sites to achieve economies of scale.

Central district offices generally have not attended to establishing a cohesive infrastructure for supporting school-based efforts to develop and enhance comprehensive approaches. Many have quite independent units focused on related matters (e.g., school psychology, counseling, nursing, social work, special and compensatory education, school safety, health education). There is often no overall administrative leader, such as an associate superintendent, who has the time and expertise to weave the parts together and ensure they are used effectively to support what must go on in each school. Such a leader is needed to (a) evolve the district-wide vision and strategic planning for preventing and ameliorating problems; (b) ensure coordination and integration of enabling activity among groups of schools and system wide; (c) establish linkages and integrated collaboration among system-wide programs and with those operated by community, city, and county agencies; and (d) ensure integration with instructional and management components. This leader's functions also encompass evaluation. This includes the determination of the equity of various efforts, reviewing the improvement of the quality of all mechanisms and procedures, and, of course, ascertaining how well outcomes are achieved.

School board committee on addressing barriers to learning.   As a 1998 report from the Center for Mental Health in Schools noted, most school boards do not have a standing committee that gives its full attention to the problem of how schools address barriers to learning and teaching. This is not to suggest that boards are ignoring such matters. Indeed, items related to these concerns appear regularly on every school board's agenda. The problem is that each item tends to be handled in an ad hoc manner, without sufficient attention to the "big picture." Given this, it is not surprising that the administrative structure in most districts is not organized in ways that coalesce various functions for preventing and ameliorating student problems. The piecemeal structure reflects the marginalized status of such functions and creates and maintains fragmented policies and practices. Given that every school endeavors to address barriers to learning and teaching, school boards should carefully analyze the way they deal with these functions and consider whether they need to restructure themselves to enhance cohesion of policy and practice.

Personnel Retraining at All Levels

Over the next decade, initiatives to restructure education and community health and human services will reshape the work of all pupil service professionals and others who consult with schools. Although some current roles and functions will continue, many will disappear, and others will emerge. Opportunities will arise not only to provide direct assistance, but also to play increasing roles as advocates, catalysts, brokers, and facilitators of reform and to provide various forms of consultation and in-service training. And, it should be emphasized that these additional duties include participation on school and district governance, planning, and evaluation bodies.

All who work to address barriers to student learning must participate in capacity building activity that allows them to carry out new roles and functions effectively. This means time must be made available for personnel retraining and continuing education.

One specific example of emerging demands is the call for improving intervention effectiveness through enhancing coordination and integration of health and social services. The movement toward full service schools clearly requires functions that go beyond direct service and traditional consultation (Knoff & Batsche, 1991; Reschly & Ysseldyke, 1995). More generally, as public schools struggle to deal with poor achievement and escalating psychosocial problems, there are many specific needs and opportunities related to addressing barriers to learning and enhancing healthy development that warrant greater attention. Examples include enhancing personalization of instruction and special assistance; helping schools and communities create comprehensive, integrated approaches; clarifying how to plan and implement interventions so they are more cost-effective; and supporting evaluative efforts designed to improve interventions and their cost-effectiveness (Kress, Cimring, & Elias, 1997; Lawson, 1998; Zins, Kratochwill, & Elliott, 1993).

Furthermore, systemic change also calls for new roles and functions, including those related to facilitating the processes of change (Adelman & Taylor, 1997). Reform provides both a challenge and an opportunity for consultants to move beyond a focus on a specific student's problems. In keeping with the intent of prevention, consultants can be agents for comprehensive, systemic reform and for the restructuring of education support programs and services, thereby improving the state of the art related to enhancing how schools address barriers to learning and promote healthy development. Recent work demonstrates the value of redeploying and training a cadre of pupil services personnel as change agents in moving schools toward better approaches for addressing barriers to learning (Adelman, 1993; Adelman & Taylor, 1993, 1994; Early Assistance for Students and Families Project, 1995; Lim & Adelman, 1997). Designated as *organization facilitators*, such professionals come to the work with a relevant base of knowledge and skills. In addition, because they are seen as internal agents for change, many of the negative reactions their colleagues direct at outside reformers are minimized. Additional training provides them with an understanding of the specific activities and mechanisms required for establishing and maintaining comprehensive, integrated approaches and increases their capacity for dealing with the processes and problems of organizational change.

Besides moving support staff into change agent roles, there is growing interest in identifying common skills among education support professionals so they can cover an overlapping range of intervention activity and help to fully integrate education supports into the fabric of daily school reform efforts. This is consistent with the view that specialist-oriented activity and training should be *balanced* with a generalist perspective (e.g., Henggeler, 1995). Emerging trends designed to counter overspecialization include granting waivers of regulatory restrictions and enhancing flexibility in the use of categorical funds. Related to this, there are proposals and pilot programs focused on cross-disciplinary training and interprofessional education to better equip service professionals to assume expanding roles and functions (Brandon & Meuter, 1995; Lawson & Hooper-Briar, 1994; Research and Training Center on Family Support and Children's Mental Health, 1996). These trends recognize underlying commonalities among a variety of student problems and are meant to encourage expanded use of generalist strategies in ameliorating them (Carnegie Council on Adolescent Development, 1995). Also related is the intent to foster less emphasis on intervention ownership and more attention on accomplishing desired outcomes through flexible roles and functions for staff (see Adelman & Taylor, 1994; Lawson & Hooper-Briar, 1994; Lipsky & Gartner, 1992).

THE ACCOUNTABILITY DILEMMA AND EFFORTS TO DEVELOP AND SCALE-UP COMPREHENSIVE, MULTIFACETED, AND INTEGRATED APPROACHES

How effective is the intervention? Do you have data to support that approach? Where is your proof? Clearly, the prevailing cry is for specific evidence of results—usually in terms of readily measured, immediate bene-fits—and for cost containment. Although understandable in light of the unfulfilled promise of so many programs and the insatiable demands on limited resources, increasing mandates for proof of results in research and practice are producing what can be called *the accountability dilemma*.

Prevention researchers and practitioners understand they must be ac-countable for their actions and outcomes. At the same time, most have ex-perienced the dilemmas raised by premature demands for proof that ignore the complexities associated with developing and evaluating inter-ventions to address major mental health, psychosocial, and educational concerns. In these arenas, evaluation must focus on much more than gath-ering accountability data. Given the limitations of current approaches, evaluations must also help advance the state of the art related to practice and policy (General Accounting Office, 1989).

Accountability is a tool that can be used to encourage people and orga-nizations to meet appropriate standards, or it can be misused as in cases where unrealistic timelines and results are to be met. Over the past few de-cades, social, political, and economic forces pressing for accountability have increasingly demanded quick and dramatic results related to com-plex, long-standing problems. Ironically, as more and more resources are used to meet these accountability requirements, fewer resources are avail-able for improving the quality of existing interventions and doing the re-search necessary to advance the field.

The Example of School Reform

Current accountability demands related to school reform illustrate the di-lemma. In this arena, the demand is for unrealistically quick improvements in average achievement test scores (e.g., rapid score increases for large numbers of students in a school and/or school district). What makes the de-mand unrealistic is the absence of comprehensive and multifaceted ap-proaches to address barriers to learning. As suggested previously, the fail-ure of the school reform movement to adequately deal with this matter means that many schools are missing a component that is essential for rais-ing test score averages. And, the irony is that they cannot devote the time, talent, and other resources necessary for developing such a component be-cause their resources are tied up pursuing policies that stress high stan-dards, local decision making, and increased accountability as a sufficient set of reforms.

We do not mean to imply that schools do nothing to address barriers to learning. Indeed, as schools "raise the bar," it is commonplace for them to acknowledge that something more than instructional and management reforms may be needed. For example, as attempts are made to eliminate social promotion, there is increasing emphasis on the need to institute a range of prevention and learning support programs. Unfortunately, there is a considerable gap between the acknowledgement of need and the development of essential practices. And, the profound implications of all this seem lost on those influential stakeholders who establish accountability criteria. Perhaps the situation would be different if there were effective ways to hold these stakeholders accountable for the dilemmas they create by making unrealistic demands.

How Ill-Conceived Accountability Can Inappropriately Reshape Research and Practice

There are undeniable benefits from demonstrating that intended outcomes are achieved. However, if one is not careful, the desire for information on efficacy can redesign a program's underlying rationale in ways that inappropriately reduce its breadth of focus. This was the case some years ago when there was a push toward behavioral- and criterion-referenced outcomes as ways to improve instructional accountability. In too many cases, this trend resulted in the drifting away from long-range educational aims to a limited set of immediately measurable objectives. The result, as commonly happens in cases of "teaching to the test," was that many important things were ignored simply because they were not directly evaluated. To facilitate measurement of immediate results, complex aims are frequently translated into highly specific, concrete, short-term objectives. Such short-range objectives are not ends in themselves; they are a small part of a particular goal and may be prerequisites to attaining the goal. It is essential not to lose sight of the fact that many specific objectives are relatively small, unrepresentative, and often unimportant segments of the most valued aims society has for its citizens—and that citizens have for themselves. Unfortunately, in the translation to short-range, measurable objectives, the essence of some intended outcomes can be distorted, and the breadth of intervention foci can be narrowed.

Even when an outcome is not easily measured, if it is important, it still must be evaluated as well as is possible and kept in the forefront of discussions about intended results. For example, efforts to prevent learning, behavior, and emotional problems encompass concern for both reducing problems and enhancing wellness (Cowen, 1997). Wellness outcomes do not receive the attention they warrant, in part because they are not easy to measure, and this situation is unlikely to change unless a concerted effort to evaluate relevant variables is made.

As the aforementioned concerns suggest, accountability demands can and do reshape the essence of intervention research and practice (Adelman, 1986; Adelman & Taylor, 1994; Burchard & Schaefer, 1992; Cuban, 1990). Indeed, evaluation methodology has the ability to alter interventions to such a degree that the research and development focus on ameliorating major societal problems can be fundamentally undermined. Evidence of the negative impact of the pressures for quick evidence of the results is well illustrated by the narrow focus of the data reported on prevention and early intervention programs (e.g., see Albee & Gullotta, 1997; Bond & Compas, 1989; Dryfoos, 1990; Durlak, 1995; Elias, 1997; Schorr, 1988; Slavin, Karweit, & Wasik, 1994; Weissberg, Gullotta, Hamptom, Ryan, & Adams, 1997).

Unfounded Underlying Presumptions

Two unfounded presumptions are at the core of most accountability oriented evaluations in education and psychology. One premise is that any approach in widespread use must be at a relatively evolved stage of development and thus warrants the cost of summative evaluation. The other supposition is that major conceptual and methodological problems associated with evaluating program efficacy and effectiveness are already resolved. The truth, of course, is that programs are frequently introduced prior to adequate development, with a view to evolving them based on what is learned each day. And, as evaluation methodologists clearly acknowledge, the most fundamental problems related to summative evaluation have not been solved. Moreover, even when a project has demonstrated an approach's efficacy, most scaled-up efforts are poorly conceived and underfunded (Adelman & Taylor, 1997; Replication and Program Services, 1993). Thus, it is not surprising that findings from the evaluation of prevention programs that have gone to scale indicate a significant drop in effectiveness (Durlak & Wells, 1997; Elias, 1997; Sarason, 1990; Weisz, Donenberg, Han, & Weiss, 1995).

One way to deal with the dilemma is to ensure that accountability is pursued within the context of an *evaluative research* agenda. Such an agenda is essential to the development and eventual scale-up of the type of intervention continuum illustrated in Figure 1. Although there are many unresolved concerns related to evaluative research, scholarly work has advanced the way such activity is conceived in education and psychology, and thus there are ample methodological guidelines (Adelman & Taylor, 1994; Chen & Rossi, 1992; Hollister & Hill, 1995; Knapp, 1995; Pogrow, 1998; Scriven, 1993; Sechrest & Figueredo, 1993; Weiss, 1995). First and foremost is the emphasis on data gathering and analyses that can help improve the intervention. In designing such formative evaluations, the methodology also should address, as much as is feasible, immediate accountability demands and anticipate long-term summative evaluations of efficacy and effectiveness (Adelman, 1986; Adelman & Taylor, 1994).

CONCLUDING COMMENTS

As schools strive for reform, the primary emphasis is on high standards, high expectations, assessment, accountability, and no excuses. These are all laudable guidelines for reform. They are simply not sufficient. It is time for policy makers to deal more effectively with the reality that, by themselves, the best instructional reforms cannot produce the desired results when large numbers of students are not performing well. It is essential to enhance the way every school site works to prevent, and to ameliorate barriers to learning and teaching. Each school needs policy support to help evolve a comprehensive, multifaceted, and well-integrated approach for accomplishing the aim of addressing barriers and for doing so in ways that weave the work seamlessly with the school's efforts to enhance instruction and school management. Progress along these lines is hampered by the marginalized status of programs and personnel whose primary focus is on enabling learning by providing a continuum of programs and services. At school sites, central offices, and school boards there is not a comprehensive focus on this arena of policy and practice because key mechanisms are missing. The absence of such structural mechanisms, along with unrealistic accountability demands, make it difficult to work powerfully and cohesively to improve how current resources are used, and hinders exploration of comprehensive and multifaceted approaches.

ACKNOWLEDGMENTS

This article was prepared in conjunction with work done by the Center for Mental Health in Schools at UCLA which is partially supported by funds from the U.S. Department of Health and Human Services, Public Health

Services, Health Resources and Services Administration, Bureau of Maternal and Child Health, Office of Adolescent Health.

REFERENCES

Adelman, H. S. (1986). Intervention theory and evaluating efficacy. *Evaluation Review, 10,* 65–83.

Adelman, H. S. (1993). School-linked mental health interventions: Toward mechanisms for service coordination and integration. *Journal of Community Psychology, 21,* 309–319.

Adelman, H. S. (1996a). Restructuring education support services and integrating community resources: Beyond the full service school model. *School Psychology Review, 25,* 431–445.

Adelman, H. S. (1996b). *Restructuring support services: Toward a comprehensive approach.* Kent, OH: American School Health Association.

Adelman, H. S., & Taylor, L. (1993). *Organization facilitator guidebook.* Los Angeles: Early Assistance for Students and Families Project. Copies available from the School Mental Health Project, Department of Psychology, UCLA.

Adelman, H. S., & Taylor, L. (1994). *On understanding intervention in psychology and education.* Westport, CT: Praeger.

Adelman, H. S., & Taylor, L. (1997). Addressing barriers to learning: Beyond school-linked services and full service schools. *American Journal of Orthopsychiatry, 67,* 408–421.

Adelman, H. S., & Taylor, L. (1998) Involving teachers in collaborative efforts to better address barriers to student learning. *Preventing School Failure, 42*(2), 55–60.

Adler, L., & Gardner, S. (Eds.). (1994). *The politics of linking schools and social services.* Washington, DC: Falmer.

Albee, G. W., & Gullotta, T. P. (Eds.). (1997). *Primary prevention works.* Thousand Oaks, CA: Sage.

Bond, L., & Compas, B. (Eds.). (1989). *Primary prevention in the schools.* Newbury Park: Sage.

Borders, L. D., & Drury, S. M. (1992). Comprehensive school counseling programs: A review for policymakers and practitioners. *Journal of Counseling & Development, 70,* 487–498.

Brandon, R. N., & Meuter, L. (1995). *Proceedings: National Conference on Interprofessional Education and Training.* Seattle: Human Services Policy Center, University of Washington.

Burchard, J. D., & Schaefer, M. (1992). Improving accountability in a service delivery system in children's mental health. *Clinical Psychology Review, 12,* 867–882.

Burt, M. R. (1998). *Reasons to invest in adolescents.* Paper prepared for the Health Futures of Youth II: Pathways to Adolescent Health. Washington, DC: Maternal and Child Health Bureau, Department of Health and Human Services.

Cahill, M. (1994). *Schools and communities: A continuum of relationships.* New York: The Youth Development Institute, The Fund for the City of New York.

Cahill, M. (1998). *Development of a core set of principles for community strategies to enhance youth health and development.* Paper prepared for Health Futures of Youth II: Pathways to Adolescent Health. Washington, DC: Maternal and Child Health Bureau, Department of Health and Human Services.

Carnegie Council on Adolescent Development. (1988). *Review of school-based health services.* New York: Carnegie Foundation.

Carnegie Council on Adolescent Development. (1995). *Great transitions: Preparing adolescents for a new century.* New York: Carnegie Corporation.

Catalano, R. F., & Hawkins, J. D. (1995). *Risk-focused prevention: Using the social development strategy*. Seattle, WA.: Developmental Research and Programs, Inc.

Center for Mental Health in Schools. (1996). *Addressing barriers to learning: Current status and new directions*. Los Angeles: Author.

Center for Mental Health in Schools. (1997). *Addressing barriers to learning: Closing gaps in school-community policy and practice*. Los Angeles: Author.

Center for Mental Health in Schools. (1998). *Restructuring Boards of Education to enhance schools' effectiveness in addressing barriers to student learning*. Los Angeles: Author.

Chen, H., & Rossi, P. (Eds.). (1992). *Theory-driven evaluations in analyzing policies and programs*. Westport, CT: Greenwood.

Comer, J. P. (1997). *Waiting for a miracle*. New York: Dutton.

Cowen, E. L. (1997). On the semantics and operations of primary prevention and wellness enhancement (or will the real primary prevention please stand up?). *American Journal of Community Psychology, 25,* 245–257.

Cowen, E. L., & Hightower, D. A. (Eds.). (1996). *School-based prevention of children at risk: The primary mental health project*. Washington, DC: American Psychological Association.

Cuban, L. (1990). Reforming again, again, and again. *Educational Researcher, 19,* 3–13.

Dryfoos, J. G. (1990). *Adolescents at risk: Prevalence and prevention*. New York: Oxford University Press.

Dryfoos, J. G. (1994). *Full-service schools: A revolution in health and social services for children, youth and families*. San Francisco: Jossey-Bass.

Dryfoos, J. G. (1998). *Safe passage: Making it through adolescence in a risky society*. New York: Oxford University Press.

Durlak, J. A. (1995). *School-based prevention programs for children and adolescents*. Thousand Oaks, CA: Sage.

Durlak, J. A., & Wells, A. M. (1997). Primary prevention programs for children and adolescents: A meta-analytic review. *American Journal of Community Psychology, 25,* 115–152.

Duttweiler, P.C. (1995). *Effective strategies for educating students in at risk situations*. Clemson, SC: National Dropout Prevention Center.

Early Assistance for Students and Families Project. (1995). *Guidebook*. Los Angeles: School Mental Health Project, Department of Psychology, University of California Los Angeles.

Elias, M. J. (1997). Reinterpreting dissemination of prevention programs as widespread implementation with effectiveness and fidelity. In R. P. Weissberg, T. P. Gullotta, R. L. Hamptom, B. A. Ryan, & G. R. Adams (Eds.), *Establishing preventive services* (pp. 253–289). Thousand Oaks, CA: Sage.

General Accounting Office. (1989). *Prospective evaluation methods: The prospective evaluation synthesis* (General Accounting Office/PEMD-89-10). Washington, DC: Author.

Goleman, D. (1995). *Emotional intelligence*. New York: Bantam.

Greenwald, R., Hedges, L. V., & Laine, R. D. (1996). The effect of school resources on student achievement. *Review of Educational Research, 66,* 361–396.

Henggeler, S. W. (1995). A consensus: Conclusions of the APA Task Force report on innovative models or mental health services for children, adolescents, and their families. *Journal of Clinical Child Psychology, 23,* 3–6.

Hoagwood, K., & Erwin, H. (1997). Effectiveness of school-based mental health services for children: A 10-year research review. *Journal of Child and Family Studies, 6,* 435–451.

Hollister, G., & Hill, J. (1995). *Problems in the evaluation of community-wide initiatives*. A paper prepared for the Roundtable on Comprehensive Community Initiatives. New York: Russel Sage Foundation.

Karoly, L. A., Greenwood, P. W., Everingham, S. S., Hoube, J., Kilburn, M. R., Rydell, C. P., Sanders, M., & Chiesa, J. (1998). *Investing in our children: What we know and don't know about the costs and benefits of early childhood interventions.* Santa Monica, CA: RAND.

Kazdin, A. E. (1993). Adolescent mental health: Prevention and treatment programs. *American Psychologist, 48,* 127–141.

Knapp, M. (1995). How shall we study comprehensive, collaborative services for children and families? *Educational Researcher, 24,* 5–16.

Knoff, H., & Batsche, G. (1991). Integrating school and educational psychology to meet the educational and mental health needs of all children. *Educational Psychology, 26,* 167–183.

Kress, J. S., Cimring, B. R., & Elias, M. (1997). Community psychology consultation and the transition to institutional ownership and operation of intervention. *Journal of Educational and Psychological Consultation, 8,* 231–253.

Larson, J. (1994). Violence prevention in the schools: A review of selected programs and procedures. *School Psychology Review, 23,* 151–164.

Lawson, H. A. (1998). Academically based community scholarship, consultation as collaborative problem-solving, and a collective responsibility model for the helping fields. *Journal of Educational and Psychological Consultation, 9,* 171–194.

Lawson, H., & Hooper-Briar, K. (1994). *Expanding partnerships: Involving colleges and universities in interprofessional collaboration and service integration.* Oxford, OH: The Danforth Foundation and the Institute for Educational Renewal at Miami University.

Lim, C., & Adelman, H. S. (1997). Establishing school-based collaborative teams to coordinate resources: A case study. *Social Work in Education, 19,* 266–277.

Lipsky, D. K., & Gartner, A. (1992). Achieving full inclusion: Placing the student at the center of educational reform. In W. Stainback & S. Stainback (Eds.), *Controversial issues confronting special education: Divergent perspectives* (pp. 3–12). Boston: Allyn & Bacon.

Pogrow, S. (1998). What is an exemplary program, and why should anyone care? A reaction to Slavin and Klein. *Educational Researcher, 27,* 22–29.

Replication and Program Services. (1993). *Building from strength: Replication as a strategy for expanding social programs that work.* Philadelphia: Author.

Reschly, D. J., & Ysseldyke, J. E. (1995). School psychology paradigm shift. In A. Thomas & J. Grimes (Eds.), *Best practices in school psychology—III* (pp. 17–32). Washington, DC: National Association for School Psychologists.

Research and Training Center on Family Support and Children's Mental Health (1996). *Interprofessional education for family-centered services: A survey of interprofessional/interdisciplinary training programs.* Portland, OR: Portland State University.

Rosenblum, L., DiCecco, M. B., Taylor, L., & Adelman, H. S. (1995). Upgrading school support programs through collaboration: Resource coordinating teams. *Social Work in Education, 17,* 117–124.

Sailor, W., & Skrtic, T. M. (1996). School/community partnerships and educational reform: Introduction to the topical issue. *Remedial and Special Education, 17,* 267–270, 283.

Sarason, S. B. (1990). *The predictable failure of educational reform: Can we change course before its too late?* San Francisco: Jossey-Bass.

Scattergood, P., Dash, K., Epstein, J., & Adler, M. (1998). *Applying effective strategies to prevent or reduce substance abuse, violence, and disruptive behavior among youth.* Newton, MA: Educational Development Center, Inc.

Schorr, L. B. (1988). *Within our reach: Breaking the cycle of disadvantage.* New York: Doubleday.

Schorr, L. B. (1997). *Common purpose: Strengthening families and neighborhoods to rebuild America.* New York: Anchor.

Scriven, M. (1993). *Hard-won lessons in program evaluation.* San Francisco: Jossey-Bass.

Sechrest, L., & Figueredo, A. J. (1993). Program evaluation. *Annual Review of Psychology, 44,* 645–674.

Slavin, R., Karweit, N., & Wasik, B. (1994). *Preventing early school failure: Research on effective strategies.* Boston: Allyn & Bacon.

Thomas, A., & Grimes, J. (Eds.). (1995). *Best practices in school psychology—III.* Washington, DC: National Association for School Psychologists.

Tyack, D., & Cuban, L. (1995). *Tinkering toward Utopia: A century of public school reform.* Cambridge, MA: Harvard University Press.

Urban Learning Center. (1995). *A design for a new learning community.* Los Angeles: Los Angeles Educational Partnership.

Weiss, C. H. (1995). Nothing as practical as a good theory: Exploring theory-based evaluation for comprehensive community initiatives for children and families. In J. B. Connell, A. C. Kubisch, L. Schorr, & C. H. Weiss (Eds.), *New approaches to evaluating community initiatives: Concepts, methods, and concepts.* Washington, DC: Aspen Institute.

Weissberg, R. P., Gullotta, T. P., Hamptom, R. L., Ryan, B. A., & Adams, G. R. (Eds.). (1997). *Establishing preventive services* (pp. 253–289). Thousand Oaks, CA: Sage.

Weisz, J. R., Donenberg, G. R., Han, S. S., & Weiss, B. (1995). Bridging the gap between laboratory and clinic in child and adolescent psychotherapy. *Journal of Consulting and Clinical Psychology, 63,* 699–701.

Zins, J. E., Kratochwill, T. R., & Elliott, S. N. (Eds.). (1993). *Handbook of consultation services for children.* San Francisco: Jossey-Bass.

APPENDIX

SIX INTERRELATED CLUSTERS OF ENABLING ACTIVITY

I. Classroom Focused Enabling

When a teacher has difficulty working with a youngster, the first step is to address the problem within the regular classroom and perhaps with added home involvement. The emphasis is on enhancing classroom-based efforts that enable learning by increasing teacher effectiveness for preventing and handling problems. Personalized help is provided to increase a teacher's array of strategies for working with a wider range of individual differences. For example, teachers learn to use volunteers and peer tutoring to enhance social and academic support and to increase their range of accommodative strategies and their ability to teach students compensatory strategies. As appropriate, support *in the classroom* is provided by resource and itinerant teachers and counselors. Work in this area requires (a) programs for personalized professional development; (b) systems to expand resources; (c) programs for temporary out of class help; and (d) programs to develop aides, volunteers, and any others who help in classrooms or who work with teachers to enable learning. Through classroom-focused enabling programs, teachers are better prepared to address similar problems when they arise in the future. (The classroom curriculum already should encompass a focus on fostering socioemotional and physical development; such a focus is seen as an essential element in preventing learning, behavior, emotional, and health problems.) Besides enabling learning, two aims of all this work are to increase mainstreaming efficacy and reduce the need for special services.

II. Student and Family Assistance

Student and family assistance should be reserved for the relatively few problems that cannot be handled without adding special interventions (e.g., health and social services, special education). The emphasis is on providing special services in a personalized way to assist with a broad range of needs. To begin with, available social, physical and mental health, and remedial programs in the school and community are used. As community outreach brings in other resources, they are linked to existing activity in an integrated manner. Special attention is paid to enhancing systems for triage, case and resource management, direct services to meet immediate needs, and referral for special services and special education resources and placements as appropriate. Ongoing efforts are made to expand and enhance resources. Work in this area requires (a) programs designed to support classroom focused enabling, with specific emphasis on reducing the need for teachers to seek special programs and services; (b) a stakeholder information program to clarify available assistance and how to access help; (c) systems to facilitate requests for assistance and strategies to evaluate the requests (including the use of strategies designed to reduce the need for special intervention); (d) a programmatic approach for handling referrals; (e) programs providing direct service; (f) programmatic approaches for effective case and resource management; and (g) interface with the community outreach to assimilate additional resources into current service delivery. As major outcomes, the intent is to ensure that special assistance is provided when necessary and appropriate and that such assistance is effective.

III. Crisis Assistance and Prevention

Schools must respond to, minimize the impact of, and prevent crises. This requires (a) systems and programs for emergency and crisis response at a site, throughout a school complex, and community wide (including a program to ensure follow-up care) and (b) prevention programs for school and community to address school safety and violence reduction, suicide prevention, child abuse prevention, and so forth. Desired outcomes of crisis assistance include ensuring that immediate emergency and follow-up care is provided so that students are able to resume learning without undue delay. Prevention activity outcomes are reflected in indexes that show there is a safe and productive environment and that students and their families have the type of attitudes and capacities needed to deal with violence and other threats to safety.

IV. Support for Transitions

A variety of transitions concerns confront students and their families. A comprehensive focus on transitions requires planning, developing, and maintaining (a) programs to establish a welcoming and socially supportive school community, especially for new arrivals; (b) counseling and articulation programs to support grade-to-grade and school-to-school transitions, moving to and from special education, going to college, moving to post school living and work; and (c) programs for before and after-school and for intersession to enrich learning and provide recreation in a safe environment. Anticipated outcomes are reduced alienation and increased positive attitudes and involvement related to school and various learning activities.

V. Home Involvement in Schooling

Work in this area includes (a) programs to address specific learning and support needs of adults in the home, such as ESL classes and mutual support groups; (b) programs to help those in the home meet their basic obligations to the student, such as instruction for parenting and for helping with schoolwork; (c) systems to improve communication about matters essential to the student and family; (d) programs to enhance the home–school connection and sense of community; (e) interventions to enhance participation in making decision that are essential to the student; (f) programs to enhance home support related to the student's basic learning and development; (g) interventions to mobilize those at home to problem solve related to student needs; and (h) intervention to elicit help (support, collaborations, and partnerships) from those at home with respect to meeting classroom, school, and community needs. The context for some of this activity may be a *parent center* (which may be part of a *Family Service Center* facility, if one has been established at the site). Outcomes include indexes of parent learning, student progress, and community enhancement specifically related to home involvement.

VI. Community Outreach for Involvement and Support (Including a Focus on Volunteers)

Outreach to the community is to build linkages and collaborations, develop greater involvement in schooling, and enhance support for efforts to enable learning. Outreach is made to (a) public and private community agencies, universities, colleges, organizations, and facilities; (b) businesses and professional organizations and groups; and (c) volunteer service programs, organizations, and clubs. Activity includes (a) programs to recruit community involvement and support (e.g., linkages and integration with community health and social services; cadres of volunteers, mentors, and individuals with special expertise and resources; local businesses to adopt-a-school and provide resources, awards, incentives, and jobs; formal partnership arrangements); (b) systems and programs specifically designed to train, screen, and maintain volunteers (e.g., parents, college students, senior citizens, peer and cross-age tutors and counselors, and professionals-in-training to provide direct help for staff and students—especially targeted students); (c) programs outreaching to hard-to-involve students and families (those who do not come to school regularly, including truants and dropouts); and (d) programs to enhance community–school connections and a sense of community (e.g., orientations, open houses, performances and cultural and sports events, festivals and celebrations, workshops and fairs). Outcomes include indexes of community participation, student progress, and community enhancement.

Howard S. Adelman is a Professor of Psychology and Codirector of the School Mental Health Project and its national Center for Mental Health in Schools at UCLA. His research and teaching focuses on young people in school settings who manifest learning, behavior, and emotional problems. In recent years, he has been involved in systemic reform and scale-up initiatives to enhance school and community efforts to address barriers to learning and enhance healthy development.

Linda Taylor is a Clinical Psychologist for the Los Angeles Unified School District and Codirector of the School Mental Health Project and its national Center for Mental Health in Schools at UCLA. Throughout her career, she has focused a wide range of psychosocial and educational problems experienced by children and adolescents. Currently, she is involved with systemic reform initiatives designed to weave school and community efforts to address barriers to learning and enhance healthy development more effectively.

JOURNAL OF EDUCATIONAL AND PSYCHOLOGICAL CONSULTATION, 11(1), 37–64

Implementation and Diffusion of the Rainbows Program in Rural Communities: Implications for School-Based Prevention Programming

Laurie Kramer, Gary Laumann, and Liesette Brunson
University of Illinois at Urbana-Champaign

Although progress has recently been made in the development of effective prevention programs for children and families, the effective diffusion of programs has received much less attention. Rural communities in particular may face unique barriers in taking advantage of prevention programs. Through a qualitative case study of the implementation of the *Rainbows program*, a prevention program for children experiencing parental separation, divorce, or death, this article explores school, family, and community resources that may affect the adoption and implementation of this program in rural schools. Perspectives on these issues were shared by 21 school personnel from a single educational region in individual or focus group interviews. Based on these perspectives, a number of recommendations are advanced for enhancing program diffusion, for furthering research on diffusion issues, and for helping educational and psychological consultants bring prevention into the educational mainstream.

Recent decades have brought great progress in the development of effective preventive intervention programs for children and families. However, issues involved in the effective implementation and diffusion of programs

Correspondence should be addressed to Laurie Kramer, Department of Human and Community Development, University of Illinois, 1105 W. Nevada, Urbana, IL 61801. E-mail: l-kramer@uiuc.edu have received much less attention. Just as program content may need to be tailored to meet the diverse needs of different groups of consumers, adjustments in how a given program is delivered may be necessary to ensure that programs are available to all in need (Cowen et al., 1996; Durlak, 1995). This issue becomes critical for program delivery in communities that have few resources. Rural communities that have few socioeconomic and educational resources may be less able to adopt programs and to sustain them over time (Wagenfeld, Murray, Mohatt, & DeBruyn, 1994). Creative approaches are needed to support low-resource communities as they take on new programs. Through a qualitative case study of the implementation of the *Rainbows program,* a prevention program for children who have experienced parental separation, divorce or death, this article explores the school, family, and community resources that may affect the adoption of this program in rural schools.

PREVENTION PROGRAMS FOR CHILDREN
EXPERIENCING PARENTAL DIVORCE OR DEATH

There is a pressing need for programs that can help children adjust to the loss of access to a parent through separation or divorce. Over 1 million children experience the divorce of their parents each year in the United States (U.S. Bureau of the Census, 1992). According to the U. S. Bureau of the Census (1999), in 1996 approximately 28% of all children lived with just one parent, which is a significant increase from 1970 (Shiono & Quinn, 1994).

As Amato and Keith (1991) demonstrated in their meta-analysis of 95 studies on the effects of divorce, most children undergoing a divorce transition are not beset with serious problems (i.e., suicide, depression, delinquency). However, most children of divorce do experience emotional pain and confusion (Emery, 1994; Emery & Forehand, 1994). Children of divorce may also be affected by experiences related to predivorce family dysfunction, such as repeated exposure to high levels of interparental conflict, experiences that may be even more potent than the effects of parental separation itself (Amato, Loomis, & Booth 1995; Block, Block, & Gjerde, 1996; Emery, 1994; Grych & Fincham, 1990, 1992; Hetherington, Bridges, & Insabella, 1998; Johnston, Kline, & Tschann, 1991; Katz & Gottman, 1993; Long, Slater, Forehand, & Fauber, 1988). Thus, it may be most accurate to consider divorce as a series of events that create a number of stressors that children must negotiate to maintain their sense of well-being (Emery, 1994; Emery & Forehand, 1994). Children's need for support increases when their families experience discord, when they lose support from a parent (e.g., when parents are focused on their own grief), and when their families face additional stressors secondary to loss. Outside resources may be needed to help children obtain the support they need to maintain well- being during the divorce transition (Emery, 1994).

Although the loss of a parent because of death is very different from loss because of marital separation (and occurs much less frequently), this event is also a critical transition that confronts children with a series of emotionally laden demands. Similar to divorce, parental grief may lessen the support children receive from their remaining parent. Sandler et al. (1992) showed that children are most vulnerable to long-term psychological difficulties after parental death if they also experience less parental warmth, greater parental demoralization, more negative life events, and an unstable family environment. Thus, children who experience loss because of parental death may also benefit from outside supportive resources.

Preventive intervention programs offered through schools have the potential to help large numbers of children who have experienced loss of access to a parent through separation, divorce, or death. Durlak (1995) estimated that large-scale, school-based prevention programs could potentially double the number of children who are helped compared to those currently reached through traditional channels of mental health intervention. In addition to increasing the number of children served, school-based prevention programs may offer several advantages. First, because school-based programs usually do not charge families for their services, children from low-income homes are more likely to enroll (Cowen et al., 1996; Grych & Fincham, 1992). Second, parents who are uncomfortable seeking help from a mental health center may agree to a school-based program because the school context is familiar to them (Cowen et al., 1996). Additional advantages of school-based programs include the availability of teachers and counselors who can help children adjust to family changes (Cowen, Hightower, Pedro-Carroll, Work, & Wyman, 1989; Kalter et al., 1988) and can offer the opportunity to practice new coping skills with peers undergoing similar experiences (Teja & Stolberg, 1993). Finally, locating programs in schools may increase the long-term availability of programs if schools incorporate the program and offer it on an ongoing basis (Cowen et al., 1989). Although the advantages of school-based prevention programs are generally viewed as outweighing the disadvantages (Durlak, 1995), it should be noted that, because schools are often required to fulfill a myriad of mandates, they may be less able than other community institutions to provide prevention services.

PROGRAM DIFFUSION

It is not enough to develop good programs for children; they must be adopted and maintained over time. According to Durlak (1995), the diffusion of a school-based program can be divided into four phases:

1. Dissemination, in which schools are informed about the existence and operation of a new program.
2. Adoption, in which a school decides to try a new program.
3. Implementation, in which the school conducts the program.
4. Maintenance, in which the program is incorporated into the routine operations of the school.

However, program developers and evaluators have devoted little attention to the factors that promote or inhibit the diffusion of programs at each of these stages (Adelman & Taylor, 1997; Durlak, 1995). The failure to attend to program diffusion issues may mean that effective programs are not available to schools, resulting in many children not receiving needed help. A lack of attention to how a program was implemented may also undermine the valid evaluation of its effectiveness.

The failure of schools to adopt and maintain effective programs may have pronounced effects for children in rural contexts, particularly given the relative paucity of traditional mental health providers in rural communities (Ad Hoc Rural Mental Health Provider Work Group, 1997). Even if traditional mental health services are available, the higher levels of poverty and unemployment in rural areas may make it difficult for rural families to afford these services (Miller, 1993; Weiss & Correa, 1996). For these reasons, the consequences of the weak diffusion of school-based programs may be quite serious in rural communities.

PROGRAM EFFECTIVENESS

Most research attention has focused on the effectiveness of prevention programs, rather than the on factors that affect the success of their implementation. Several programs for children of divorce have been found to provide benefits for children of divorce: the Children of Divorce Developmental Facilitation Group (Kalter, Pickar, & Lesowitz, 1984), the Divorce Adjustment Program (Stolberg & Cullen, 1983; Stolberg & Garrison, 1985), and the Children of Divorce Intervention Program (Cowen et al., 1996; Pedro-Carroll & Cowen, 1985). Fewer programs have been developed for children who have experienced the death of a parent (Lutzke, Ayers, Sandler, & Barr, 1997) and only one—The Family Bereavement Program (Sandler et al., 1992)—is recognized as an empirically supported program. However, by far one of the largest programs serving children of divorce and death is the Rainbows program (Yehl-Marta & Olbrisch, 1997), and it has never been formally evaluated.

BACKGROUND OF THE CURRENT STUDY

This study explores factors that affect the implementation of the Rainbows program, a prevention program designed for children who are either currently experiencing social and psychological difficulties or who are at risk for developing such difficulties after parental, separation, divorce, or death. The 20-session program is most often provided as a pull-out service in elementary and middle schools. Similar to other prevention programs, the developers of the Rainbows program (Yehl-Marta & Olbrisch, 1997) have not formally articulated the theoretical underpinnings of their program. However, through a series of discussions and the review of program materials, we were able to identify the mechanisms by which the Rainbows program administrators and staff believe the program accomplishes its mission of facilitating healing among grieving children. First, through a process of mutual help, children learn empathic listening skills and practice receiving and extending help to one another in the support groups. Second, through a process of identifying and reframing cognitions, emotions, and behaviors, children are encouraged to express their feelings and to move toward acceptance of their current life situation in which loss is reconceptualized as an "ending" that will be followed by a new "beginning" (Yehl-Marta & Olbrisch, 1997).

   Although it is unusual for a single program to serve children experiencing divorce as well as parental death, the program developers (Yehl & Laz, 1983) reasoned that both groups of children go through a grieving process and need similar forms of support and assistance to cope with family change. Although the specific events that follow parental divorce and death are quite different, the program developers believed that children in both situations require similar forms of assistance from supportive adults and peers in understanding and expressing their feelings, accepting help, reframing loss, and developing coping skills. Further, through a series of age-appropriate activities, children are helped to apply the concepts taught in the Rainbows program to their unique situation.

The Rainbows program has been adopted in over 7,000 sites in 14 nations and has served over 750,000 children since its development in 1983. Although the Rainbows program is most often implemented in schools, the program has also been offered by churches, agencies, and hospitals. In each of these contexts, sponsoring institutions, rather than families, are asked to cover program costs. Secular and religious versions have been developed, and the program is also available in languages other English.

The program depends on thousands of volunteers to fill various roles in the implementation of the program at the site and regional levels. At the site level, the program is administered to groups of children by program facilitators (typically social workers, and less commonly, counselors and teachers). Site coordinators (ideally experienced program facilitators) supervise the administration of the program in a particular school by recruiting, supervising, and supporting program facilitators; enlisting participants; and acquiring resources, such as space, time, and program materials. Regional directors recruit new sites, train site coordinators and program facilitators, and supervise the administration of the program at a regional level. The RAINBOWS, Inc., headquarters develops program materials and provides ongoing training and support to regional directors. Because program personnel typically have advanced degrees in social work, counseling, or education, the training process is relatively brief: 6 hr of initial training and 10 hr of ongoing supervision and support for program facilitators, 9 hr for site coordinators, and 40 hr for regional directors.

Laurie Kramer and Gary Laumann have been involved in an ongoing evaluation of the outcome of the Rainbows program for fourth-, fifth-, and sixth-grade students who are participating in a school-based, secular version of the program. The purpose of this evaluation is to investigate whether children demonstrate higher levels of personal adjustment, report a greater sense of support, and are more able to articulate their feelings and thoughts about loss and family change as a function of participating in Rainbows program in contrast to a control group.

The process of performing this evaluation research proved to be as interesting as our findings. Early in the project we were struck by the fact that, despite a desire to adopt the Rainbows program, several rural schools were simply unable to do so. For example, with respect to a single educational region in central Illinois, 51 schools were offered the program, and 20 of these accepted. Although it is not unusual for schools to decline to participate in a project involving a substantial research component, we were intrigued by the response of eight of the schools—all rural schools—who initially made concrete plans to implement the Rainbows program (e.g., by sending a representative to a training session), but found themselves unable to follow through, although program materials and staff training were provided free of charge as part of the evaluation. An interest in exploring the reasons for this phenomenon led to the current investigation of factors that influence the implementation of the Rainbows program in rural communities.

METHOD

Design, Sampling Strategies, and Participants

A qualitative, case study method was used to investigate the factors that facilitated and impeded implementation of the Rainbows program within the rural areas of one educational region in east central Illinois. The boundaries of the region defined the boundaries of the case, and all schools and administrative offices within the region were considered part of the case.

Within the defined boundaries of the case, a theoretical sampling approach (Glaser & Strauss, 1967; Taylor & Bogdan, 1984; see also Stake, 1994) was used to select school personnel to participate in individual or focus group interviews. Theoretical sampling involves selecting informants based on the likelihood that they will provide a rich source of information about the phenomenon under study. A focus on decision making in the adoption and implementation of the Rainbows program led us to select individuals who had a role in determining whether and how a particular program will be introduced in a school. In the region under study, a number of individuals were involved in the implementation process:

1. Regional and district administrators who "give their blessing" for individual schools to accept a particular program.
2. School principals who play a "gatekeeping" role in determining whether the program is actually offered in their particular school.
3. School personnel with responsibility for implementing and coordinating prevention programs (e.g., school social workers).

Knowledgeable individuals who worked at each of these levels were referred to us by the regional school superintendent. (Most of these individuals were also known to us through the execution of the outcome evaluation.) With the exception of four social workers who were unable to come to a focus group interview, all invited individuals agreed to be interviewed.

The total number of participants was 21. At the regional level, we interviewed the regional superintendent and the 4 regional administrators involved in making decisions about new school programs ($n = 5$). At the local administrative level, we interviewed local administrators from 2 of the 5 rural districts in which at least one school offered the Rainbows program, and 4 of the 8 rural districts that did not offer the Rainbows program ($n = 6$). With respect to school personnel with responsibility for implementing and coordinating the program, we conducted a focus group interview with 9 of the 11 social workers who, working through a special education cooperative, delivered services in 10 of the 13 rural districts. One additional social worker who was not a part of the regional cooperative, but who worked in one of the remaining rural districts, was also interviewed. (Although 6 staff members from the 2 urban districts in the region were initially invited to participate in a separate focus group to provide a basis for rural–urban comparisons, the participation rate for this group [$n = 2$] was too low to warrant inclusion in this study.) In sum, we were able to talk with everyone with responsibility for prevention programming at the regional administrative level, to local administrators from 6 of the 13 rural districts, and to school staff with program delivery responsibilities in 11 of the 13 rural districts in the region.

Data Collection

Data were collected by using individual and focus group interviews. Individual interviews were scheduled with regional, district, and individual school-level administrators, and a focus group interview was conducted with school social workers. Because school administrators were expected to make decisions about program implementation after considering the particular needs and resources of their school and the surrounding community, the individual interview format was thought to be most effective for exploring these unique perspectives in depth. On the other hand, a focus group discussion format was felt to be most appropriate for assessing the perspectives of individuals most likely to serve in the role of site coordinators and program facilitators (e.g., school social workers), given that these individuals would share a similar role in implementing programs in their schools.

In both individual and focus group interviews, participants were presented with a small set of open-ended questions. Specifically, participants were asked:

1. Whether it was difficult to implement programs targeted to children experiencing parental separation, divorce, or death, and if so, why?

2. Whether program implementation was more difficult in rural rather than in urban locations, and if so, why?
3. What would help them to implement, or better implement, this type of program in their schools?

Those participants who did not implement the Rainbows program were first asked to reflect on the factors that influenced their decisions regarding the Rainbows program in particular, and then encouraged to reflect more generally on barriers in the implementation of similar prevention programs. A standard set of probes was used to help respondents elaborate on their responses. Field notes and audiotape recordings from these interviews formed the basis for subsequent data analysis.

Data Analysis

Three general strategies were used to enhance the rigor of the qualitative analysis of the research interviews (Kalafat & Illback, 1998; Lincoln & Guba, 1985). First, as is desirable with qualitative analysis, the researchers were substantially grounded in the phenomenon of interest. Two of us have had extensive involvement with both the Rainbows program and its implementation in this educational region. Laurie Kramer contracted with RAINBOWS, Inc., to design and conduct the outcome evaluation described previously. Gary Laumann had been involved with the implementation of the Rainbows program in numerous school districts in Illinois for 8 years, most recently serving as regional director for east central Illinois. He introduced the Rainbows program to the schools in this region (and others), worked with each participating school to implement the program, and trained the site coordinators and program facilitators. Following procedures recommended by Krueger (1994), Liesette Brunson, a researcher with interests in rural families and prevention, was invited to participate in the data analysis and write-up as an outside source of peer checking. Thus, the research team was substantially grounded in the setting of interest and brought to bear multiple areas of expertise in delivering school-based prevention services to rural families.

Second, data analyses were conducted following Krueger's (1994) model for analyzing focus group interviews and Taylor and Bogdan's (1984) procedures for discovery of themes in qualitative data. Specifically, we used a tape-based analysis (Krueger, 1994) that involved the systematic review of tape-recorded interview material and the construction of a framework or "story line" with which to integrate the major themes in the data.

Third, we employed two levels of participant checks. First, we asked participants to respond to key points during the interview situation, with the interviewer presenting a summary of themes that emerged during the interview and requesting feedback, qualification, and elaboration from participants. Second, we mailed a preliminary report of discovered themes to all of the research participants and asked them to comment. These comments, which ranged from a few scribbled lines in the margins of the report to a two-page memo, were incorporated into the results.

RESULTS

This section presents the characteristics of schools, families, and communities reported by the participants in this study as influencing whether the Rainbows program was adopted and maintained in the rural schools of this educational region. Before presenting these results, it is important to consider the following caveats.

First, the results represent the viewpoints of the participants and should not be interpreted as objective facts. Second, because the participants were selected for their involvement in different levels of roles in relation to program adoption and implementation, their comments were considered as analogous to puzzle pieces in which each participant group provided input about unique facets of the problem. In piecing together this puzzle, we did not place greater weight on the comments made by administrators over those made by social workers, or vice versa. We did attempt to assess whether a particular viewpoint was expressed by several participants in diverse roles, by several participants in a particular role, or by only one or two participants, and we indicate this finding in the text. Third, although strong and consistent themes emerged across the participants' reports, it is important to consider that there are individual differences among schools and communities, particularly in their demographic characteristics and resources (Prater, Bermudez, & Owens, 1997), that limit the degree to which any specific theme can be said to apply to a particular school or community. For example, rural communities vary significantly in terms of the residential stability of their population, their financial assets, and their proximity to suburban and urban centers. Each of these factors (as well as many others) may have substantial impact on the resources and constraints existing in a school or district.

FACTORS AFFECTING PROGRAM ADOPTION AND IMPLEMENTATION

Participants discussed a wide range of factors that may have influenced whether the Rainbows program was adopted and was sustained in rural schools. One consistent theme related to the types of resources (personnel, time, space, and attitudes) needed to make program adoption successful. These resources were based in the contexts of schools, families, and communities.

School Resources

Personnel.   One important school-based resource that was uniformly reported by informants to influence implementation of the Rainbows program was the availability of key personnel to coordinate and conduct the program. Social workers were the school personnel who most often took responsibility for administering the Rainbows program in their schools, although this type of program delivery was not part of their "official" job description. Social workers reported that they took on this additional responsibility because they recognized a great need for it. However, this commitment came at a cost because they were already overloaded with responsibilities, such as case study reports, crisis intervention, and counseling. Furthermore, their time in a particular school was constrained by the structure of social work services in rural schools in the region. Unlike the urban schools in the region that had a half- or full-time social worker on staff, all but one rural school purchased part-time (typically 1 day per week) social work services from a county Special Education Cooperative. This arrangement, which resulted in an individual social worker working in four or five schools during a single week, was viewed as significantly impeding program coordination. One social worker described the practical implications of this arrangement: "With me in the school only 1 day a week, it could take until Thanksgiving to give out and get back the consent forms for the program." Some social workers viewed this arrangement as impeding their ability to become integrated into the fabric of the school and its surrounding community, which in turn limited their effectiveness in implementing the Rainbows program.

A second, staff-related constraint discussed was the difficulty identifying school personnel other than social workers who could implement the Rainbows program. In general, rural schools in the region were (accurately) reported to have a smaller staff than were urban schools. School administrators pointed out that small staff size yields fewer degrees of freedom for adopting innovations, especially those intended to meet special needs. Virtually all participants noted that rural schools in the region faced challenges in maintaining a full complement of staff. In fact, positions for counselors, psychologists, librarians, and special education teachers in these rural schools often remained vacant for several years, leaving existing school staff to pull "double duty" to cover some of these functions. Teachers were rarely thought to be in the position to take on programming responsibilities because of inflexibility in their classroom teaching schedules. School administrators pointed out that because of new retirement incentives in the state, a rural school's faculty may be largely composed of novice teachers. Although generally enthusiastic, these teachers were viewed as offering less support to program delivery efforts because their energy was invested in learning how to be teachers. Furthermore, many young teachers left rural schools—before becoming experienced enough to contribute to programs such as the Rainbows program—for better paying positions in urban and suburban communities.

A final factor thought to affect the recruitment of individuals to deliver the Rainbows program was the availability of professional development activities that promote the value of prevention to school staff. Social workers and school administrators both felt that opportunities for professional development were less available to personnel in the region's rural schools. This was viewed as a serious limitation, especially if staff members had not received prior training on how schools could contribute to prevention efforts. Although the Rainbows program includes staff training, participants felt that individuals who took advantage of the Rainbows program training were those who already believed in the value of prevention.

Time and space. In addition to staffing limitations, restricted resources in terms of time and space were viewed by participants as critical factors that inhibited the implementation of the Rainbows program in their rural schools. Finding an appropriate space that allowed for confidentiality to conduct the program was reported to be challenging. Similarly, problems were reported in finding a time to offer the program. Transportation arrangements made it difficult to schedule sessions before or after school because children could not miss their buses. Furthermore, administrators and social workers reported that teachers were understandably reluctant to have children miss class (or even recess) to participate. Integrating the program into classroom activities was not seen as a potential solution because teachers felt that the prescribed curriculum was too difficult to cover in the time they had. Most Rainbows program facilitators in the region resolved this problem by giving up their lunch time to offer the program.

Finances.   An additional constrained resource that was viewed as hampering the adoption of the Rainbows program was money. This topic was more often discussed by regional district administrators than by school-level personnel. Although the administrators recognized that urban schools in the region also faced financial challenges, they felt that because rural schools generally operate from a smaller tax base than do urban schools, there was often less money to purchase prevention programs and to cover some of the "hidden" costs associated with their implementation, such as funds for hiring substitute teachers and paying stipends to allow teachers to attend training sessions. As one program administrator pointed out, "there is not a line item in the budget for prevention. No money is expressly set aside for buying and maintaining prevention programs." Despite these financial concerns, several administrators made it clear that they were quite willing to bear these costs if a program was thought to be important enough and if staff members were committed to implementing the program.

Receptivity toward innovations.   A final school-based resource that was viewed as affecting the adoption of the Rainbows program was the "culture" of the school and its attitude toward innovations. Participants consistently described their rural schools, in comparison to urban schools, as representing a more closed culture in that the influx of new ideas and practices were more limited. One regional administrator described the difference as follows: "Just the number and diversity of individuals walking through the school's doors every day differs in rural and urban schools."

The issue of schools' receptivity towards innovations was perceived to be related to an underlying question of what the mission of modern schools should be. Participants indicated that schools in the region face contradictory imperatives from their communities. On the one hand, there is a strong pressure to improve student achievement. The school, the community, or both may adopt a "no frills" attitude that the mission of the school should be strictly focused on academics and not social services. There may also be a corresponding belief that only families have the responsibility to address children's personal and social needs and that this arena is not the school's responsibility. On the other hand, there is a demand to actively promote children's social and emotional well-being. Superintendents and principals reported that schools are being called on to do more and more to support children; for example, they now must provide drug, delinquency, and violence prevention programs. However, new mandates are not necessarily accompanied by greater resources, causing schools in the region to greet new mandates with hesitation.

Family Resources.   Participants also indicated that a family-based resource—family support for the program—was particularly important for the adoption of the Rainbows program. School social workers were most vocal about the factors that affected families' ability to support prevention programs such as the Rainbows program. According to social workers, many of the rural families in their schools who needed prevention services were not clamoring for them. From their perspective, it was more common for rural families to draw upon their endogenous support systems for help rather than to turn to "outsiders" or the Rainbows program. These attitudes were thought to follow from concerns about privacy and confidentiality, as well as from the belief that meeting children's needs is a family rather than a school responsibility. Social workers felt that families' concerns about privacy were often exacerbated by school personnel's role of mandated reporter; social workers emphasized that low income and minority families often equate school social workers with state child protection agents and so may mistrust school-based programs for fear of being accused of child abuse or neglect.

Many participants also mentioned that families' support of the Rainbows program may be limited by a fear of stigmatization. School social workers raised the issue that many parents perceive that the role of a social worker is to assist children who have mental health problems. Thus, parents with this view may be fearful that their child's participation in the Rainbows program would be interpreted by the school and the community as indicating that the child had emotional problems or that the family was dysfunctional. Children were thought to have similar fears; social workers felt that children sometimes worried that their peers would assume they were experiencing psychological difficulties if they left their classroom with a social worker. Social workers also felt that some families were reluctant to acknowledge any adjustment difficulties that their children did experience. They suggested that because some families had fled to rural communities to get away from what they perceived as urban problems (e.g., substance abuse, violence in the community, or racial or other disharmony), they may resist acknowledging any problems, even if their child was grieving, reasoning that, "we came to this town to get away from these problems," or that, "my child doesn't need this type of service."

Participants also felt that family stress often had the paradoxical effect of distancing children from school-based programs. Regional administrators and several school social workers believed that parents facing multiple difficulties may be less willing to enroll their child in the Rainbows program because they are unaware of the program (because they were uninvolved in the school), too overwhelmed to help their child access the program, or mistrustful of school programs in general. Social workers and superintendents reported that some communities in the region were experiencing an influx of low income families who had moved from urban areas because housing costs are lower. Some of these families were perceived to bring problems, such as poverty, substance abuse, domestic violence, and peer violence with them. Participants felt that the irony of this situation was that these families were moving from urban communities, which were thought to have more resources, to communities that had markedly fewer resources. School-based support was thought to be critical because of this lack of alternative, community-based services.

Community Resources

Community receptivity: Will it play in Peoria—or rather Peotone? Several respondents, particularly those at the administrative level, considered the explicit support of the community, or at least its key leaders, as a necessary resource for successful program adoption. The words of one of regional administrator aptly captured a view generally held by participants, that fostering the acceptance of a new program is analogous to marketing a new product:

> When you bring a new product on line you need to be sure that all your sales reps are on board and on line to sell. You need to align your resources with the needs of the district. It's difficult to stay on top of this since you have to be sensitive to the changing political events of the community.

Participants felt that community acceptance was enhanced when key community players were recruited to help market the program. Principals and superintendents, especially those new to a district, were described as being unwilling to introduce the Rainbows program if they were not confident about community receptivity.

Volunteerism.   Given the difficulties in staffing rural schools, the volunteer base of rural communities was perceived to be a potential resource for bolstering programs such as the Rainbows program. However, the volunteer base of rural communities was described by school administrators as diminished in comparison to past decades. They attributed this, in part, to the reduced role of farming in rural communities, a factor that has prompted young adults to move away from rural communities and forced parents of school-aged children to take work in suburban or urban areas, leaving less time for volunteerism. Furthermore, local administrators pointed out that, even when volunteers were available, liability and security issues made them reluctant, and sometimes unwilling, to accept their help. This was especially true of volunteers not personally known to the administration and those unable to make a long-term commitment to the school. Administrators reported that background checks, which can take a substantial period of time, were now routinely required of all volunteers.

Community structures and supports.   Participants felt that a third important, but underused, community-based resource for supporting the Rainbows program was assistance from community social service agencies. According to school administrators and social workers, there were limited opportunities for schools in rural communities to collaborate with external agencies in ways that would support programming, for example, through consultation or staff training services. Instead, school social workers reported that the main existing connection between rural schools and external agencies took the form of referrals for individual children. They attributed this limited collaboration to three factors:

1. Relevant agencies tended to be based in distant urban areas.
2. Schools may mistrust external agencies because of bad experiences. (e.g., Some agencies have not been forthcoming with information or have left schools in vulnerable positions.)
3. There were no school personnel with explicit responsibility for maintaining relationships with external agencies.

In response to a probe about whether university-based resources might fill some of the gaps in community-based support, regional school administrators reported that schools were often reluctant to enter into relationships with university personnel because historically such help was offered in a "top down," rather than in a collaborative, way. In the words of one regional administrator,

The university ... would come in and try to do something, and they weren't there for the long haul; they wanted to do research on kids; they wanted to utilize kids.... They weren't interested in the kids—they were interested in the project—to get research.

Despite these barriers, several regional administrators viewed the situation as having recently improved, at least with regard to collaborating with this specific university, and were optimistic that university-based interns and research services could benefit their schools and support the implementation of the Rainbows program.

Implementors Versus Nonimplementors

The viewpoints of decision makers who had expressed an interest in the Rainbows program but were not able to implement the program were given particular attention in our analyses. Although the topics raised by these individuals did not differ significantly from those who worked in schools where the Rainbows program was successfully implemented, some issues were emphasized more strongly. Staff time was consistently mentioned by nonimplementors as the most expensive resource inhibiting program implementation in their schools. As one administrator described the situation, even when staff were excited about the program, crucial questions remained: "When are you [the staff members] going to meet with the students, and what are you *not* going to do instead?"

Additional factors mentioned by nonimplementors included the need for the Rainbows program to fit into a coordinated, long-term plan for the school as a whole, and competition of the Rainbows program with a large number of other programs that also promised to meet key needs. With respect to the latter issue, one administrator mentioned that the opportunity to offer the Rainbows program competed with programs he felt had lesser value, but that there was little information available to help sort the worthwhile from less useful programs.

FACTORS AFFECTING PROGRAM MAINTENANCE

Despite a direct question addressing program maintenance, it was interesting that the majority of responses from participants related to program adoption. However, some participants addressed the resources they perceived as most critical for supporting the ongoing provision of the Rainbows program. One school administrator described the problem of program maintenance as one in which the school must incorporate the program into its system:

> In a smaller [school] system, human resources are spread thin and pulled in different directions. It is hard to develop a new initiative under these conditions. It takes time to have it be incorporated. They [the staff] have to grow into it, internalize it, make it their own. The program needs to have meaning to the staff before it's accepted.

The most common factor noted by school social workers and principals as inhibiting program maintenance was related to staff fatigue and burnout. Because, in this region, the Rainbows program is often administered and implemented by a single individual, the program could collapse if this individual left the school or experienced significant life stress. Participants felt that it was essential to eventually bring in additional people who could share responsibility for the program.

Family support was also viewed as important for program maintenance. Sustained participation and positive feedback from families was thought to be needed to confirm to the school that children were getting something out of the program. An enthusiastic response from families was also viewed as important for preventing staff burnout.

Finally, many of the participants mentioned that continued community support may be important to ensure that resources exist for recurring program needs. However, few specific suggestions as to how specific community resources could directly contribute to their school's ongoing programming efforts were offered.

PARTICIPANTS' RECOMMENDATIONS FOR PROGRAM ADOPTION AND MAINTENANCE

Participants made several recommendations about how resources could be better used or developed to support the adoption and maintenance of the Rainbows program. Most of these recommendations addressed two key issues: (a) how to build and maintain support for programs, and (b) how to support school staff who deliver programs.

How to Build and Maintain Support for the Rainbows Program

1. Demonstrate program effectiveness.   Social workers and administrators felt that demonstrations of program effectiveness were needed to maintain support for the program. Evaluations performed at the local level were viewed as critical because the school (and the community) wants to see that the Rainbows program is working with *their* children in *their* schools. Evaluations that tie program gains to academic achievement, or to the reduced likelihood of substance abuse or violence, were viewed as having the most positive impact. Evaluation data were also thought to be useful for providing administrators with critical data for distinguishing between programs of varying quality.

2. Identify a champion.   Principals can sometimes be convinced to adopt the Rainbows program if a key staff member is enthusiastic about the program and is willing to serve as its "champion," for example, by promoting the program to school staff, children, and families and by assuming responsibility for program coordination. However, participants stressed that even with an identified champion, a program will not survive if the principal is not supportive.

3. Nurture a culture of prevention.   As new school staff are hired, they need to be trained and mentored to appreciate the value of prevention and the school's expanded role. This could occur through in-service activities (offered perhaps by community social service agencies, university partners, or the Rainbows program registered directors) and mentoring relationships with staff experienced in delivering prevention programs. The development of mechanisms for retaining teachers who are interested in prevention should receive greater attention.

4. Build and highlight family support.   Families could be encouraged to request the Rainbows program from the school. Parents could be informed about the Rainbows program through various venues, such as mandatory divorce education classes for divorcing parents, pediatricians, hospice, or community mental health centers. Superintendents' and principals' concerns about accepting the program may be lessened if they receive proactive messages from the community about the program's desirability.

5. Increase communication with parents.   Personal   communication with parents about how the program could help their children could be increased. Social workers suggested that they may be more effective in reaching potential program participants if they and classroom teachers approach families in a sensitive manner to describe how their child might benefit from the Rainbows program. In addition to the existing practice of inviting parents to an informational presentation about the Rainbows program, participants thought that communication with parents could also be enhanced through newsletters and handouts that include practical suggestions for promoting targeted skills at home. Participants felt that program developers should create these supportive materials.

6. Build school–family–community collaboration.   Collaboration among all stakeholders is important to integrating the Rainbows program into the school structure. One recommendation made by school administrators was to assess and build the base of existing and potential support in the community before introducing the Rainbows program. Furthermore, one regional administrator advised that collaborations among program developers, implementers, and community stakeholders should be thought of as critical interpersonal relationships that need to be nurtured.

7. Keep the program available.   Sustained program availability is important: The community needs to be able to count on the program to be there and to be available for referrals. Social workers recommended that school personnel recognize this issue at the outset so that their commitment could carry them through some of the difficult times. For example, even if only one child participated in the Rainbows program in a given year, staff could remind themselves of the importance of keeping the program going, so it would be available to those who need it in future years.

8. Keep the program visible.   Familiarity breeds acceptance. Better advertising and promotion could be used to enhance program awareness and acceptance. Social workers advised that program developers should "keep the program in front of us—we accept what is commercially promoted."

How to Support School Staff who Deliver the Program

1. Develop more than one program advocate.   To avoid burnout, it is imperative that programming duties not persistently rest on the shoulders of a single individual.

2. Provide ongoing support.   Although the Rainbows program model does include ongoing support of program facilitators by site coordinators, additional training and consultation could be provided by individuals associated with the program developers (e.g., registered directors of the Rainbows program), by outside consultants (e.g., partners from community service organizations or university), or by school personnel who are employed to promote programming efforts. To acknowledge that these are valued professional development activities, staff should receive a stipend for participating in training. Training needs to occur at times and locations that are convenient to staff.

3. Use volunteers or interns as appropriate.   Staff overload can also be relieved by community volunteers and interns. Even if it is not possible or advisable for volunteers to run the Rainbows program group because of confidentiality and liability issues, they could still help by taking over a social worker's lunchroom or bus duty so that she or he could run the program. Because of the limited availability of volunteers in rural communities, interns from a nearby college or university, who could make an extended commitment to the school, could be trained to run the program. Social workers felt that "interns would be seen as credible to parents," and furthermore, that their unfamiliarity with the families in the community may help promote the sense that confidentiality will be maintained.

4. Provide recognition and incentives.   Concrete incentives (preferably money or relief from other duties) should be offered to staff members for coordinating or implementing the program. This would give a direct message to staff that their investment in the program is valued.

DISCUSSION

Decision makers and program deliverers described a number of factors that they believed were important for the successful implementation of the Rainbows program in the rural schools in which they worked. Participants appeared to have well-developed mental maps about the school, family, and community resources that affected the implementation of the Rainbows program in their rural schools.

Concrete resources, such as personnel, child referrals, time, relief from other duties, recognition, and reward, were thought to flow more easily if the base of support within a school was well established. In schools where the Rainbows program had been successfully implemented, participants described a base of support that rested firmly on the shoulders of a program champion, an individual who sees meeting the needs of children experiencing family stress as a school priority, believes in the Rainbows program as a key mechanism for addressing that need, and has the charisma needed to convince parents and other school staff of the value of the program. Despite the personal strengths of program champions and their many successes, these individuals—the base of support for the Rainbows program in rural schools—are on shaky ground. For example, the structure of service delivery in most rural schools in the region, which ensures that schools receive needed social work services despite staff shortages, has the paradoxical effect of constraining the amount of time a social worker can spend in a given school. In addition, competing work demands and a difficulty in identifying other staff members with whom to share program responsibilities threatens the long-term sustainability of the program in these schools.

The school's ability to implement the Rainbows program was also seen to depend on family and community support. Participants felt that family support was often intrinsically limited by the difficulties families were experiencing that led their children to need additional services in the first place. Community supports were seen to be missing or underused because of a history of noncollaborative relations, mistrust, or a failure to appreciate the strengths of rural schools and communities.

The perspectives advanced by participants in this research, in many cases, parallel themes in the existing literature that point to the unique needs of rural communities with respect to prevention efforts. These perspectives echo the factors identified by Helge (1981) as hindering the adoption of special education programming in rural areas; specifically (a) teacher retention and recruitment problems; (b) rural attitudinal problems, such as resistance to change; and (c) problems based on rural geography. Results from this study are also consistent with previous research in highlighting the fact that program diffusions do not occur automatically. Instead, diffusion efforts must be carefully planned and implemented with significant effort from multiple individuals in complementary roles working in collaboration (Adelman & Taylor, 1997, 1998; Durlak, 1995).

The results of the present study extend beyond previous research in offering a set of recommendations advanced by experienced program implementors for facilitating the implementation of the Rainbows program in rural schools. Many of these recommendations focused on ways to remediate the problems that stemmed from limited personnel in rural schools. For example, participants felt that, ideally, program implementation would be enhanced if prevention activities were expressly included in school budgets and if one or more staff members could be hired to select and coordinate programs, train staff to implement programs, and work to support the evaluation of programs. However, at present, this does not appear to be a growing trend. A recommendation that may have a greater likelihood of being enacted in some rural schools to counter personnel limitations is the development of linkages with university-based resources (e.g., interns, research services). Recommendations such as these reflect many of the suggestions made by Reaves and Larmer (1996) on how the unique problems associated with professional development training in rural schools can be remedied through collaboration with university partners.

Educational consultants may be in a critical position to help support school-based prevention efforts. Educational consultants can help achieve the vision of bringing prevention into the educational mainstream in several ways by:

1. Contributing to professional development efforts in school districts.
2. Providing guest lectures in college and university training programs for teachers, social workers, and administrators on the value of prevention.
3. Preparing articles on prevention in educational contexts for regional and statewide professional newsletters.
4. Networking with, and enhancing connections between, professionals who have common interests in prevention in the hope that there is strength in numbers.
5. Becoming an active voice in local school affairs.
6. Leading or participating in evaluations that demonstrate local effectiveness (Small, 1996).
7. Providing school decision makers with information that will help them to distinguish between prevention programs of varying quality.

All of these efforts can provide a forum for changing the overall climate of accepting and prioritizing prevention programs in the schools.

It is important to be aware of the limitations of the present research. One limitation is that no information is provided about how accurate participants' mental models of the factors affecting program implementation were. We can note that the themes we discerned in participants' responses seldom contradicted each other; often corroborated each other; and where not matching, appeared to contribute different facets to a full picture. However, these data do not provide any basis for determining accuracy. The consistency among reports could well reflect a shared understanding built over time, rather than correspondence with reality. A potential area for future research is to use the factors that appear in the mental maps of participants to generate hypotheses about the factors that influence program adoption. For example, it remains to be seen whether rural schools are more resistant to change—more so than in urban schools—in ways that reduce the likelihood that prevention programs would be adopted. Similarly, the respondents consistently pointed out that support from families and communities are important for the successful implementation of programs such as the Rainbows program, yet representatives from those groups were not interviewed to check the veracity of these statements. Hypotheses such as these should be investigated in future research.

Although retaining some skepticism for how participants' views may or may not be accurate, we still recognize that their views influence how they act within the systems in which they are embedded. Thus, a second area for further research is to investigate the process decision makers engage in as they assess support for innovation and as they determine what tools and strategies can be used to enhance this process. For example, it is interesting to note that participants seemed to have the least well-developed mental maps about the factors that influence family and community support for the Rainbows program. An investigation of families' perspectives on how school-based prevention programs do and do not meet their and their children's needs, and what influences their support of such programs, seems particularly needed and useful. Providing service providers with an enhanced understanding of service recipients' experiences should help to enhance communication between schools and families. Similarly, the investigation of how community organizations perceive school efforts toward prevention could help build linkages that may, in the long run, result in new mechanisms for helping children in need.

A second important limitation of these findings is the questionable validity of some of the specific comparisons participants drew between rural and urban schools. Although respondents felt that rural schools in the region were often at a greater disadvantage for accepting and maintaining prevention programs, this conclusion is in fact an empirical question not addressed by this research. Similarly, whether this conclusion is applicable to all rural schools is also an empirical question not addressed by this research. Prior research indicates that a great deal of diversity exists among rural schools (Knight, Knight, & Quickenton, 1996), suggesting that some rural schools and communities may be well positioned to accept prevention programs, whereas others may be poorly positioned. Adelman and Taylor (1998) also point out that many of the restrictions in rural schools' resources described by participants also characterize some urban and suburban schools. We suspect that many of these resource constraints, rather than being *unique* to rural schools, are simply *common* in many rural schools and may also be common in other schools with resources that are constrained by factors such as poverty and discrimination. Similarly, the degree to which the current results are generalizable to other school-based prevention programs is not known. Future research could also examine how limited resources affect the implementation of different prevention programs, in both rural and urban contexts, and whether certain strategies are effective in addressing resource restrictions.

In conclusion, RAINBOWS, Inc., has been tremendously successful in having their program implemented worldwide. We hope that some of the strategies identified in this research will facilitate the program's implementation in rural schools in particular, and in schools with fewer resources in general. It is important to acknowledge that in addition to serving children in need, RAINBOWS, Inc., as well as other organizations with similar successful programs, offer researchers important opportunities to study the factors involved in implementation and diffusion. We encourage researchers to take greater advantage of opportunities such as these.

ACKNOWLEDGMENTS

This project was funded by the University of Illinois Rural Families Program which is sponsored by the Illinois Council for Food and Agricultural Research, and RAINBOWS, Inc. Portions of this article were presented as part of the symposium, "Programming for Rural Families and Communities: Challenges and Policy Implications," coordinated by Ellen Abell, at the annual conference of the National Council of Family Relations, November 1998, Milwaukee, WI.

REFERENCES

Ad Hoc Rural Mental Health Provider Work Group. (1997). *Final report of the Ad Hoc Rural Mental Health Provider Work Group.* Rockville, MD: U.S. Department of Health and Human Services.

Adelman, H. S., & Taylor, L. (1997). Toward a scale-up model for replicating new approaches to schooling. *Journal of Educational and Psychological Consultation, 8,* 197–230.

Adelman, H. S., & Taylor, L. (1998). Reframing mental health in schools and expanding school reform. *Educational Psychologist, 33,* 135–152.

Amato, P. R., & Keith, B. (1991). Parental divorce and the well-being of children: A meta-analysis. *Psychological Bulletin, 110,* 26–46.

Amato, P. R., Loomis, L. S., & Booth, A. (1995). Parental divorce, marital conflict, and offspring well-being during early adulthood. *Social Forces, 73,* 895–915.

Block, J. H., Block, J., & Gjerde, P. F. (1996). The personality of children prior to divorce: A prospective study. *Child Development, 57,* 827–840.

Cowen, E. L., Hightower, A. D., Pedro-Carroll, J. L., Work, W. C., & Wyman, P. A. (1989). School-based models for primary prevention programming with children. In R. Lorion (Ed.), *Prevention in human services* (Vol. 7, pp. 133–160). Binghamton, NY: Haworth.

Cowen, E. L., Hightower, A. D., Pedro-Carroll, J. L., Work, W. C., Wyman, P. A., & Haffey, W. G. (1996). *School-based prevention for children at risk: The primary mental health project.* Washington, DC: American Psychological Association.

Durlak, J. A. (1995). *School-based prevention programs for children and adolescents.* Newbury Park, CA: Sage.

Emery, R. E. (1994). *Renegotiating family relationships: Divorce, child custody, and mediation.* New York: Guilford.

Emery, R. E., & Forehand, R. (1994). Parental divorce and children's well-being: A focus on resilience. In R. J. Haggerty, N. Garmezy, M. Rutter, & L. Sherrod (Eds.), *Risk and resilience in children* (pp. 64–99). Cambridge, England: Cambridge University Press.

Glaser, B. G., & Strauss, A. L. (1967) *The discovery of grounded theory.* Chicago: Aldine.

Grych, J. H., & Fincham, F. D. (1990). Marital conflict and children's adjustment: A cognitive-contextual framework. *Psychological Bulletin, 108,* 267–290.

Grych, J. H., & Fincham, F. D. (1992). Interventions for children of divorce: Toward greater integration of research and action. *Psychological Bulletin, 111,* 424–454.

Helge, D. I. (1981). Problems in implementing comprehensive special education programming in rural areas. *Exceptional Children, 47,* 514–520.

Hetherington, E. M., Bridges, M., & Insabella, G. M. (1998). What matters? What does not?: Five perspectives on the association between marital transitions and children's adjustment. *American Psychologist, 53,* 167–183.

Johnston, J. R., Kline, M., & Tschann, J. M. (1991). Ongoing post-divorce conflict in families contesting divorce: Do joint custody and frequent access help? In J. Folberg (Ed.), *Doing custody and shared parenting* (pp. 177–184). New York: Guilford.

Kalafat, J., & Illback, R. J. (1998). A qualitative evaluation of school-based family resource and youth service centers. *American Journal of Community Psychology, 26,* 573–604.

Kalter, N., Alpern, D., Falk, J., Gittelman, M., Markow, M., Okla, K., Pickar, J., Rubin, S., Schaefer, M., & Schreier, S. (1988). *Children of divorce: Facilitation of development through school-based groups* (manual). Lansing, MI: Author.

Kalter, N., Pickar, J., & Lesowitz, M. (1984). School-based intervention groups for children of divorce: A preventive intervention. *American Journal of Orthopsychiatry, 54,* 40–51.

Katz, L. F., & Gottman, J. M. (1993). Patterns of marital conflict predict children's internalizing and externalizing behaviors. *Developmental Psychology, 29,* 940–950.

Knight, J. P., Knight, C. S., & Quickenton, A. (1996). Education in rural schools. *The Education Forum, 61,* 84–89.

Krueger, R. A. (1994). *Focus groups: A practical guide for applied research.* Thousand Oaks, CA.: Sage.

Lincoln, Y. S., & Guba, E. G. (1985). *Naturalistic inquiry.* Beverly Hills, CA: Sage.

Long, N., Slater, E., Forehand, R., & Fauber, R. (1988). Continued high or reduced interparental conflict following divorce: Relation to young adolescent adjustment. *Journal of Consulting and Clinical Psychology, 56,* 467–469.

Lutzke, J. R., Ayers, T. S., Sandler, I. N., & Barr, A. (1997). Risks and interventions for the parentally bereaved child. In S. A. Wolchik & I. N. Sandler (Eds.), *Handbook of children's coping: Linking theory and intervention* (pp. 215–243). New York: Plenum.

Miller, B. A. (1993). Rural distress and survival: The school and the importance of "community." *Journal of Research in Rural Education, 9,* 84–103.

Pedro-Carroll, J. L., & Cowen, E. L. (1985). The children of divorce intervention program: An investigation of the efficacy of a school-based prevention program. *Journal of Consulting and Clinical Psychology, 53,* 603–611.

Prater, D. L., Bermudez, A. B., & Owens, E. (1997). Examining parental involvement in rural, urban, and suburban schools. *Journal of Research in Rural Education, 13,* 72–75.

Reaves, W. E., Jr., & Larmer, W. G. (1996). The effective schools project: School improvement in rural settings. *The Rural Educator, 18,* 29–33.

Sandler, I. N., West, S. G., Baca, L., Pillow, D. R., Gersten, J. C., Rogosch, F., Virdin, L., Beals, J., Reynolds, K. D., Kallgren, C., Tein, J., Kriege, G., Cole, E., & Ramirez, R. (1992). Linking empirically based theory and evaluation: The Family Bereavement Program. *American Journal of Community Psychology, 20,* 491–521.

Shiono, P. H., & Quinn, L. S. (1994). Epidemiology of divorce. *The Future of Children, 4*(1), 15–28.

Small, S. A. (1996). Collaborative, community-based research on adolescents: Using research for community change. *Journal of Research on Adolescence, 6,* 9–22.

Stake, R. (1994). Case studies. In N. Denzin (Ed.), *Handbook of qualitative research* (pp. 236–247). Thousand Oaks, CA: Sage.

Stolberg, A. L., & Cullen, P. M. (1983). Preventive interventions for families of divorce: The divorce adjustment project. In L. A. Kurdek (Ed.), *New directions in child development: Vol. 19. Children and divorce* (pp. 71–81). San Francisco: Jossey-Bass.

Stolberg, A. L., & Garrison, K. M. (1985). Evaluating a primary prevention program for children of divorce. *American Journal of Community Psychology, 13,* 111–124.

Taylor, T. J., & Bogdan, R. (1984). *Introduction to qualitative research methods.* New York: Wiley.

Teja, S., & Stolberg, A. L. (1993). Peer support, divorce, and children's adjustment. *Journal of Divorce and Remarriage, 20,* 45–64.

U. S. Bureau of the Census. (1992). *Statistical Abstract of the United States* (112th ed.). Washington, DC: Government Printing Office.

U. S. Bureau of the Census. (1999). Child suppport for custodial mothers and fathers: 1995. *Current population reports* (pp. 60–196). Washington, DC: Government Printing Office.

Wagenfeld, M. O., Murray, J. D., Mohatt, D. F., & DeBruyn, J. C. (1994). *Mental health and rural America: 1980-1993. An overview and annotated bibliography.* Washington, DC: U.S. Department of Health and Human Services.

Weiss, K. E., & Correa, V. I. (1996). Challenges and strategies for early childhood special education services in Florida's rural schools: A DELPHI study. *Journal of Research in Rural Education, 12,* 33–43.

Yehl, S., & Laz, M. (1983). *Rainbows* (manual). Schaumberg, IL: RAINBOWS, Inc.

Yehl-Marta, S., & Olbrisch, L. (1997). *Rainbows* (manual). Rolling Meadows, IL: RAINBOWS, Inc.

Laurie Kramer is an Associate Professor of Applied Family Studies in the Department of Human and Community Development at the University of Illinois at Urbana-Champaign. Her research interests include family coping with life transitions, family conflict, and children's sibling relationships.

Gary M. Laumann is a doctoral candidate in Human Development and Family Studies at the University of Illinois at Urbana-Champaign. His research interests include family transitions and the development and evaluation of prevention programs. He is also the registered regional director of the Rainbows program in east central Illinois.

Liesette Brunson is Coordinator of Research Programs for the Illinois Rural Families Program at the University of Illinois at Urbana-Champaign. Her research interests include understanding community resources that promote resilience in rural areas.

JOURNAL OF EDUCATIONAL AND PSYCHOLOGICAL CONSULTATION, 11(1), 65–92

Building Full-Service Schools: Lessons Learned in the Development of Interagency Collaboratives

Thomas J. McMahon, Nadia L. Ward, Marsha Kline Pruett, Larry Davidson, and Ezra E. H. Griffith
Yale University School of Medicine

Although the history of clinical–school–community collaboration can be traced back to the end of the 19th century, the full-service school movement represents a new era in the quest for more effective ways to deliver human services to children. Building on the personal experience of the authors and the literature concerning the development of integrated service delivery systems, this article outlines conceptual, administrative, fiscal, legal–ethical, and practical issues that can hinder local efforts to develop full-service schools. The systematic analysis of potentially negative influences is presented as something that must be pursued by educational and psychological consultants so that, as the next millennium begins, they will be in a position to help local working groups develop interagency collaboratives that more effectively integrate school and human service systems, increase service use, and promote positive developmental outcomes for children living in high-risk situations.

Although the history of clinical–school–community collaboration can be traced back to the end of the 19th century, the full-service school movement represents a new era in the quest for more effective ways to deliver human services to children. As awareness that school systems alone cannot address the social problems affecting millions of children, the concept of full-service schools has been embraced as a potential solution to service delivery problems affecting children living in high-risk environments. Built

Correspondence should be addressed to Thomas J. McMahon, Yale University School of Medicine, Department of Psychiatry, West Haven Mental Health Clinic, 34 Park Street, New Haven, CT 06519. E-mail: thomas.mcmahon@yale.edu on shared commitment to positive child development, full-service schools represent an effort to make human service systems partners in the educational process, while simultaneously making school systems partners in the delivery of human services (Adelman & Taylor, 1999; Dryfoos, 1994a, 1995, 1997, 1998; Morrill, 1992).

Despite growing enthusiasm about comprehensive systems of school-based intervention, it is important to note that the concept of full-service schools emerged in the midst of longstanding ambivalence about the presence of human service professionals in the schools, recurrent problems in the implementation of school-based programs, and failure to move new ideas past the demonstration phase of development (Dryfoos, 1994a; Flaherty, Weist, & Warner, 1996; Sedlak, 1997; Tyack, 1992). Although innovative partnerships described by Dryfoos (1994a, 1995, 1997, 1998) and others (e.g., Eber & Nelson, 1997; Holtzman, 1992, 1997; Zigler, Finn-Stevenson, & Stern, 1997) reflect substantial interest in the integration of school and human service systems, most school buildings in this country have not yet been transformed into full-service schools. For the most part, local school systems have not yet become an integral part of the human service system; human service systems have not yet established a presence in local schools; and efforts to create full-service schools have been hindered by an array of conceptual, administrative, fiscal, legal–ethical, and practical issues.

Consequently, building on the literature concerning the development of integrated service delivery systems for children, we outline important lessons learned in our efforts to develop full-service schools designed to better meet the needs of urban teens that is at greatest risk for school failure. However, rather than simply describing the development of yet another full-service school project, we attempt to support the implementation of the concept by exploring issues that have hampered our efforts to define, develop, and evaluate interagency collaboratives. After an historical review of clinical–school–community collaboration, we define the concept of a full-service school and then discuss 10 potential barriers to implementation encountered at the local level. *From the beginning, it is important to acknowledge that our intent is not to discourage efforts to pursue the concept.* Instead, our hope is that this analysis will provide consultants joining local work groups with an outline of potential problems that must be considered in the successful implementation of all full-service school programs. By clearly delineating the factors thwarting growth, we hope to stave off premature disillusionment with a worthwhile concept that is easy to embrace but difficult to translate into day-to-day activity that improves service delivery for children.

HISTORICAL BACKGROUND

Historical precursors to contemporary community–school collaboration can be traced back to the end of the 19th century when medical practitioners began working with school staff to develop procedures for the identification and education of children with special needs (Fagan, 1985; Sedlak, 1997). G. Stanley Hall is often credited with beginning the child study movement that, in 1899, led to creation of the Department of Scientific Pedagogy and Child Study in Chicago, the first school-based child study clinic in the country (Fagan, 1985). Soon thereafter, Lightner Witmer founded the Psychological Clinic at the University of Pennsylvania and began a process of clinical–school collaboration that is still relevant to contemporary practice (Fagan, 1996). At approximately the same time, Arnold Gesell brought clinical expertise from his academic position at Yale University to an appointment as state inspector of special school children for the Connecticut Board of Education, a position historians commonly recognize as the first school psychology position in the country (Fagan, 1987a, 1987b).

Soon after the turn of the century, social work and nursing services also began appearing in the schools (Sedlak, 1997; Tyack, 1992). Whereas the child study movement evolved out of concern for children with developmental difficulties, the school social work and school nursing movements evolved out of concern about the impact of urban poverty on children. In 1902, Lina Lavanche Rogers began work in New York City as the first school-based nurse in this country, and the role of the school nurse has evolved over more than 90 years as a specialty within the field of public health nursing (Hawkins, Hayes, & Corliss, 1994). At the same time, settlement houses and the school board in New York City joined forces in 1906 and defined the concept of the *visiting teacher*, a school-based charity worker who provided social services to troubled children within the context of a school–community partnership that marked the beginning of school social work as a profession.

Between 1930 and 1960, three important paradigm shifts then contributed to movement away from community–school collaboration (Sedlak, 1997; Tyack, 1992). First, support professionals became part of the educational bureaucracy as school psychology, school nursing, and school social work became distinct educational professions. For the most part, collaboration with community providers ended as school systems retained professionals to provide support services from within the system. Second, the influence of psychoanalysis contributed to movement away from concern about social policy and system reform toward concern about clinical theory and the remediation of deficits within individuals. Third, as World

War II ended and newly married couples began leaving the city, the focus on support for children affected by urban poverty gave way to concern about the growing population of children living in the more affluent suburbs.

Following institutionalization of support services, the Rehabilitation Act of 1973 and the Education of the Handicapped Act of 1975 guaranteed school-age children with handicapping conditions access to a broad range of special services. Despite efforts to do so within projects like the School Development Program (Haynes & Comer, 1996) and the Memphis City Schools Mental Health Center (Paavola, Hannah, & Nichol, 1989), this legislation never led to broader mandates making support services available to all students. In fact, many observers (e.g., Flaherty et al., 1996; Sedlak, 1997) believe legal mandates to serve special education students contributed to significant restriction of access to support services for children without handicapping conditions as school systems struggled to fulfill legal obligations to an expanding population of students with special needs.

During the following decade, school health clinics began appearing in middle and secondary schools throughout the country (Dryfoos, 1994a). Originally designed to make primary health and family planning services available to youth living in urban settings, the need for complementary mental health, substance abuse, and social services quickly became evidence as school-based clinics became operational (Adelman, Barker, & Nelson, 1993; Dryfoos, 1994b). Conceptual models of school health programs being advanced by the Centers for Disease Control and Prevention (Kolbe, Collins, & Cortese, 1997) recognized the need for mental health and social services, but many critics (e.g., Adelman & Taylor, 1993, 1997a; Allensworth, Lawson, Nicholson, & Wyche, 1997; Short & Talley, 1997) have argued that school health clinics have never adequately accommodated the demand for psychological and social services.

THE CONCEPT OF FULL-SERVICE SCHOOLS

As the first 100 years of clinical–school–community collaboration came to a close, the concept of full-service schools emerged from this historical process as the latest strategy to more effectively deliver human services to children. Evolution of the concept was shaped by two driving forces: (a) renewed concern about social problems affecting learning and (b) intense political pressure to reorganize school, health care, and social service systems. Throughout the literature (Carlson, Paavola, & Talley, 1995; Carlson, Tharinger, Bricklin, DeMers, & Paavola, 1996; Dryfoos, 1994a, 1998;

Morrill, 1992; Paavola et al., 1996; Talley & Short, 1996), the concept of full-service schools has repeatedly been linked with (a) demands for educational reform, (b) the reorganization of health care systems, (c) renewed interest in interagency collaboration, and (d) an emerging focus on the concept of service integration. Although some observers (e.g., Adelman & Taylor, 1997a, 1999; Dryfoos, 1998) have argued that true collaboration and true integration have not yet been realized, most observers (e.g., Adelman & Taylor, 1999; Adelman et al., 1999; Dryfoos, 1994a, 1998; Paavola et al., 1996; Talley & Short, 1996) believe paradigm shifts that will eventually promote large-scale development of full-service schools are clearly underway.

According to Dryfoos (1994a, 1995, 1998), the term *full-service school* was first used in 1991 when the Florida legislature provided funding to support a system of interagency collaboratives with mandates to make a comprehensive package of human services available in school buildings. In her writing, Dryfoos (1994a) defined the full-service school as a concept to guide the organization of service delivery systems designed to promote the physical, emotional, social, and academic growth of children living in high-risk environments. From her perspective, the concept represents an ideal that integrates educational reform and the reorganization of community-based services so that children receive the best education possible, with access to the full complement of human services needed to address threats to optimal child development.

More than anything else, the concept of full-service schools represents a commitment to a specific value system and a specific strategy for service delivery. Five related principles appear to be guiding the development of these interagency collaboratives. First, the concept acknowledges the validity of increasingly sophisticated developmental–ecological models of psychosocial adjustment that characterize both positive and negative outcomes as the end result of a complex interaction of risk and protective factors present in the lives of children (see Davidson, Pruett, McMahon, Ward, & Griffith, in press). Second, the concept recognizes the problems disenfranchised families have accessing quality services and the potential to quickly increase access by moving services to school buildings because most children in this culture attend school on a daily basis (Dryfoos, 1994a).

Third, the concept of full-service schools also recognizes the need to bring a full complement of human services into the schools (Adelman & Taylor, 1998, 1999). From this perspective, full-service schools are the vehicle with which to better organize the patchwork of preventive, social, and clinical services presently delivered in school settings into an integrated continuum of interventions that range from primary prevention to intensive, community-based treatment for serious, persistent problems. Fourth, the concept embraces the need for interagency collaboration and service integration (Paavola et al., 1996). Because neither the schools nor any other agency can provide the full range of services needed to adequately address social, emotional, and behavioral barriers to learning, the concept calls for the creation of interagency networks committed to true collaboration and true integration of services. Finally, the concept of full-service schools emphasizes the importance of community (Dryfoos, 1994a, 1998; Holtzman, 1997). Community involvement in the development and maintenance of these new educational institutions is valued and actively pursued.

Since the concept of full-service schools emerged, there have been numerous descriptions of successful programs that illustrate operationalization of these five guiding principles. Dryfoos (1994a, 1995, 1997, 1998), more than anyone else, described the growing number of successful partnerships being developed across the country. Throughout her commentary on the full-service school movement, she has highlighted programs being developed through competitive bidding for public funds available in California, Florida, Kentucky, and New Jersey. Repeatedly, she has also described an array of innovative projects being supported by a number of philanthropic foundations interested in the reform of educational, health care, and social service systems.

In one of the early references on the topic, Holtzman (1992, 1997) described the School of the Future being developed in Texas with support provided by the Hogg Foundation for Mental Health. Several authors (e.g., Adelman et al., 1999; Dryfoos, 1997; Illback, Kalafat, & Sanders, 1997; Phillips, Boysen, & Schuster, 1997) have also written about the projects being supported by the School-Based Youth Service Program of New Jersey and the Kentucky Education Reform Act. Eber and Nelson (1997) also highlighted efforts to develop school-based systems of wraparound services for children, and Zigler et al. (1997) described the *School of the 21st Century*, a school–community partnership designed to move quality child care and family support services into school buildings. Most recently, Davidson et al. (in press) outlined the development of a full-service alternative high school for inner-city teens who are at greatest risk for school failure, and Garrison, Roy, and Azar (1999) described an innovative, culturally sensitive program targeting Latino youth.

Although descriptions of existing programs are relatively common, and the number of programs seems to be growing, it is not clear exactly how many full-service schools there are in this country (Dryfoos, 1998). The comprehensive accounting of activity recently done by Dryfoos (1998) suggests that, at best, most states have a limited number of programs concentrated in poor, urban school districts. Because of publicly funded initiatives (for a review, see Dryfoos, 1998), programs seem to be most common in the states of California, Florida, Kentucky, and New Jersey. New York City also seems to have a number of publicly and privately funded projects (Dryfoos, 1998). Regardless of where they are located, most programs are relatively new. Few have been in existence for more than 10 years (Dryfoos, 1998), formal evaluation of projects considered successful is just beginning (e.g., see Eber & Nelson, 1997; Holtzman, 1997; Zigler et al., 1997), and what evaluative work has been done is not readily accessible because most of it has only been published in project reports with limited circulation (for a review, see Dryfoos, 1998).

For the most part, the development of new projects is currently being guided by descriptions of existing programs (e.g., Eber & Nelson, 1997; Holtzman, 1992, 1997; Zigler et al., 1997), generic outlines of the implementation process (e.g., Calfee, Wittwer, & Meredith, 1998), and secondary review of local evaluations (e.g., Dryfoos, 1998; Eber & Nelson, 1997). Lessons learned during other efforts to reform service delivery systems (e.g., Allensworth et al., 1997; Annie E. Casey Foundation, 1995; Bickman, 1996; Cowen et al., 1996; Cross & Saxe, 1997) have also proven helpful. In general, there appears to be consensus (e.g., Adelman & Taylor, 1997a, 1999; Dryfoos, 1998; Eber & Nelson, 1997; Weist, 1997; Zigler et al., 1997) that the available data suggest that, despite being difficult to develop and institutionalize, full-service schools have the potential to promote a better interface of school and human service systems, increase service use, and positively affect developmental outcomes for children living in high-risk situations.

LESSONS LEARNED

Despite agreement about the promise of this new approach to service delivery, there has been little systematic analysis of the factors hampering local efforts to define, develop, and evaluate full-service schools. Consequently, with the hope that careful analysis of potential barriers to implementation will *support* expansion of local initiatives and define issues that need to be considered in continued evaluation of new and existing programs, we review 10 problems that have hindered our efforts to establish full-service schools in an urban setting. These potential barriers include (a) questions about what to build, (b) decisions about how to begin, (c) local politics, (d) fiscal matters, (e) gravel in the collaborative process, (f) need for positive community–school relations, (g) parallel rather than integrated administrative structures, (h) legal and ethical considerations, (i) links between school attendance and access to services, and (j) unrealistic expectations in the evaluative process.

Structures and Prototypes: What to Build?

As local planning groups begin exploring options for the development of full-service schools, they must decide what to build and how to go about building them (Adelman & Taylor, 1997b). Within the literature, some authors (e.g., Adelman, 1993; Adelman & Taylor, 1997b) have called for the description, implementation, and testing of conceptual models that can then be replicated in other settings. At this time, broad conceptual models that can be adapted to local circumstance have been developed, and replication of specific approaches has begun (for a review, see Dryfoos, 1998). For example, the School of the 21st Century, first described by Zigler in 1987, has been successfully replicated nation wide in more than 400 schools (Zigler et al., 1997). Similarly, the School of the Future supported by the Hogg Foundation for Mental Health has been successfully defined, developed, and replicated in four urban school districts in Texas (Holtzman, 1997). School-based systems of wraparound care based on the principles outlined by Eber (Eber & Nelson, 1997) are also being developed across the country, and the Children's Aid Society is currently working to replicate the success of Intermediate School #216, a settlement house located within a public middle school serving a poor, largely Dominican neighborhood in New York City (Dryfoos, 1998).

Unfortunately, although descriptions of specific projects (e.g., Eber & Nelson, 1997; Holtzman, 1992, 1997; Levy & Shepardson, 1992; Zigler et al., 1997) offer local planning groups examples of different approaches being replicated across the country, they provide little detail concerning the design, implementation, and effectiveness of these demonstration projects. Elements of the guiding principles can be found in all descriptions of full-service schools, but information about the structural elements and day-to-day operation of specific programs is much more difficult to secure. Structurally, most programs include a governance structure, an instructional component, and a support or enabling component (Adelman & Taylor, 1997a, 1998, 1999; Dryfoos, 1994a). However, after that, the structure and operation of most programs is dictated, to a large extent, by local need. Existing projects can provide local work groups with a conceptual model and guiding principles, but most observers (e.g., Dryfoos, 1994a; Gardner, 1992) agree that there is no single prototype that can be built again and again across settings, and most observers (e.g., Adelman & Taylor, 1997a; Melton, 1997) agree that the absence of conceptual distinctions and detailed information about structure and operation is hampering the development of new programs.

Even when existing models seem appropriate for implementation in other settings, some authors (e.g., Levy & Shepardson, 1992) have raised important questions about wholesale pursuit of replication. With very few exceptions, most demonstration projects have not been thoroughly evaluated, even fewer have been systematically replicated, and information about successful replication is very limited. Furthermore, as Melton (1997) pointed out, initial development and successful replication involve entirely different sets of tasks. Successful implementation in one setting does not mean replication is possible in another. Therefore, as local planning groups consider adopting conceptual models associated with specific demonstration projects, they should pursue as much information as possible about the potential utility of the approach in their community, the effectiveness of the existing project, the extent to which it has been replicated, and the availability of technical assistance.

Moreover, when planning programming for specific populations, local work groups should know that replication of an existing model may not be an option because demonstration projects that have targeted similar populations may simply not exist. For example, very little has been written about full-service alternative schools for teens at greatest risk for school failure (Davidson et al., in press), and programs in urban settings are much more common than programs in rural or suburban settings (Dryfoos, 1998). The movement also values the concept of cultural sensitivity (Dryfoos, 1998) and Garrison et al. (1999) discussed the development of programs designed to better meet the needs of Latino youth, but there has been little discussion of culture-specific programs to target other populations of ethnic minority youth.

Hence, in most situations, local planning groups should be prepared to review the literature; carefully consider the guiding principles; identify existing structures; consult with professionals involved in a planning process; and then define conceptual models, organizational structures, and operating procedures they believe will best meet the needs of their community. As local work groups wrestle with decisions about what to build, they may also find national and state centers being established to support local efforts (for descriptions, see Adelman et al., 1999; Eber & Nelson, 1997) to be viable, readily accessible sources of technical assistance. Moreover, rather than charging forward, time spent defining and refining the initial organizational structure may be time well spent. Clearly, previous experience with

the development of these (e.g., Holtzman, 1997) and other community-based initiatives (e.g., Annie E. Casey Foundation, 1995) suggests that
the better the initial plan, the more successful the implementation.

Pursuing Plans: Where to Begin?

In addition to deciding what to build, local planning groups must also decide how to pursue their plans. Dryfoos (1994a), Adelman (1993, 1996;
Adelman & Taylor, 1993, 1997b), and Holtzman (1992, 1997) each outlined
slightly different versions of the start-up process for existing programs.
Dryfoos highlighted a community-oriented process whereby a single lead
community agency assumes responsibility for the organization and administration of the initiative. Adelman described the components of a generic
process of program development that emphasizes the central role played
by an external consultant with special training in systems change who
serves as the catalyst for the creation of the new service delivery system and
then leaves once the program has been implemented. Holtzman emphasized the importance of a local coordinator who functions as a facilitator
during the planning and implementation phases and then continues as the
project director once the program is operational. Again, just as there is no
universal structural model, there is no single, best model of the planning
and implementation process. Each of these approaches has been used to begin successful programs, and there currently are no empirical data to support the use of one approach over another.

Therefore, as local work groups consider what might best meet their
needs, they should consult with professionals who have used different approaches and carefully consider the potential advantages and disadvantages of each approach. For example, the concept of a single lead agency
that can organize fiscal and administrative functions under one roof may
have appeal in some settings, but that approach should only be pursued
with awareness that there is potential for the process to derail if that
agency becomes an overbearing force (Gardner, 1992; Jehl & Kirst, 1992).
Likewise, the concept of an organizational facilitator who can serve as an
independent consultant and help marry knowledge of local needs provided by work groups with knowledge of systems reform may have appeal in other settings. Nevertheless, unless paid for by some third party to
the process, local planning groups must be prepared to finance the consultation, and they must proceed with awareness that, despite the best efforts
of everyone involved, the facilitator may become an integral part of a process that may just not work as well once that individual leaves. Similarly,

the success of the process whereby the facilitator during the planning phase remains as the project director depends on the willingness of that person to remain over an extended period of time (Holtzman, 1997). Ultimately, as with decisions about structure, available data on implementation suggest that the best strategy will be the strategy that best accommodates local circumstance.

Local Politics: All Questions are Political Questions

More than anything else, efforts to cultivate effective interagency collaboratives will highlight the extent to which political considerations can hinder their development. Given the highly competitive, highly politicized nature of school systems (for a discussion, see Crowson & Boyd, 1993), efforts to build full-service schools can quickly become the focal point of political agendas being pursued both within and across systems. Although some authors (e.g., Dryfoos, 1994a, 1998) have mentioned the potential for community opposition to the placement of services in schools, especially family planning services, there has been little discussion of other ways local politics might undermine program development. Regardless of the setting, even very sophisticated planning groups may find themselves triangulated into political struggles they must successfully negotiate if the project is to move forward.

For example, even if there is agreement that services should be located in schools, competition or outright conflict between neighborhoods may slow implementation as political factions lobby to influence which school gets chosen as the demonstration site. If politicians help secure funding for the project, they may look to showcase their involvement for political gain in ways that provoke other stakeholders and hamper the initiative. Program development may also be derailed by power struggles within the administrative structure of the school system as individuals use the project to make statements about the extent of their influence. Conflict between specific organizations or people within organizations may contribute to backroom lobbying for the exclusion of specific stakeholders, whereas concern about the preservation of tenuous relationships across agencies may dampen honest communication about areas of disagreement. In short, as planning groups begin their work, they should not underestimate the extent to which need to preserve political power, forge political alliances, or settle old scores might affect implementation of the best laid plans, and they must be prepared to quickly and effectively address political agendas that might subvert the process so that local politics do not become more important than the well-being of the children involved.

Fiscal Matters: Too Many Checks in the Mail

As the concept of full-service schools has been advanced, a number of authors (e.g., Farrow & Joe, 1992) have highlighted the extent to which local initiatives are being developed with a patchwork of local, state, and federal funding. Rather than being available without restriction, much of this support must be used in prescribed ways to address specific problems (Adelman & Taylor, 1998, 1999). In fact, some observers (e.g., Orland, Danegger, & Foley, 1997) believe that, more than anything else, the growth of full-service schools is being slowed by funding mechanisms that require school-based collaboratives secure, administer, and maintain multiple sources of categorical support. Recent use of block grants, administrative waivers, and other mechanisms that allow for more flexible use of federal and state funding may represent initial movement away from strict categorical funding of health and social services, but these changes are just beginning (Adelman et al., 1999; Adelman & Taylor, 1999; Orland et al., 1997). Until true reform of funding mechanisms occurs, the persistence of a largely categorical approach to the dissemination of public and private funds dictates that new projects develop creative mechanisms for the consolidation and management of support coming from different funding streams.

Dryfoos (1994a) recommended that a single lead agency assumes responsibility for fiscal and administrative management, and this arrangement seems to be most common among existing programs (Dryfoos, 1998). However, this strategy should only be pursued with knowledge that, despite its advantages, this approach can also create a situation where staff within that agency quickly become responsible for the generation of ongoing support. Given that most observers (e.g., Dryfoos, 1994a, 1998; Gardner, 1992) believe that the lead agency cannot be the local school system, this type of administrative structure can also lead to a situation where the school system and other parties have little financial stake in the long-term survival of the program. Despite being more difficult to create and not yet widely used, a wholly new organization established specifically to receive funding and administer the project may be an alternative to the concept of a single lead agency that ensures shared responsibility to secure and manage funding.

Furthermore, even when collaboratives develop effective mechanisms for the management of fiscal resources, the most common source of funding, funds made available specifically to support demonstration projects, may complicate the process by providing large influxes of time-limited support that must be quickly spent as stipulated in a rigid timetable. Just as limited funding can undermine an initiative, large infusions of support can also hinder development by prematurely accelerating implementation in ways that may not necessarily promote fiscal stability and long-term survival (Adelman & Taylor, 1999; Finn-Stevenson, 1992). Although all funding for demonstration projects comes with stipulations that recipients must cultivate alternative sources of support, it is difficult to institutionalize support for innovative service delivery, this rarely occurs to the extent anticipated, and projects often face substantial budget cuts as demonstration grants end (Adelman & Taylor, 1999; Melton, 1997).

As appealing as demonstration grants may be, planning groups should carefully consider the long-term impact of time-limited funds and closely examine other funding mechanisms that might support a slower, stepwise process of implementation that may actually prove more beneficial over the long-term (Finn-Stevenson, 1992). For example, as Adelman and Taylor (1998) suggested, existing patterns of external funding for school-based services can be inventoried, and school systems can be encouraged to consolidate this support into a pool of money that can be made available to support the initiative. Also, interagency agreements that begin the process can include provisions for matching funds from all organizations involved, even if those funds come primarily in the form of in-kind support for professional time, office space, utilities, supplies, and related costs (Larson, Gomby, Shiono, Lewit, & Behrman, 1992). Some authors (e.g., Armbruster, Andrews, Couenhoven, & Blau, 1999) have also highlighted the possibility of obtaining third-party reimbursement, primarily Medicaid reimbursement, for health and mental health services provided in school settings.

In addition, many observers (e.g., Dryfoos, 1998; Farrow & Joe, 1992; Gardner, 1992; Melton, 1997) have suggested that stable fiscal support is most likely to come through state mechanisms. Consistent with this position, Dryfoos (1994a, 1998) recently outlined ways state governments might support an expansion of the movement, and she described state initiatives in California, Florida, Kentucky, and New Jersey designed specifically to support the development of school-based service delivery systems. In short, the lesson here is the idea that, as collaboratives evolve, they need to consider how individual agencies might bring categorical forms of funding to the initiative as they also position themselves to pursue flexible funding made available for integrated service delivery. As local work groups begin considering potential sources of income, they should also closely follow federal efforts (for a description, see Adelman et al., 1999) to build the infrastructure to support policy analysis and fiscal planning across all levels of government, and they should be prepared to lobby state legislators for the institutionalization of funding to support the expansion of school-based collaboratives.

Building Support Teams: Grease and Gravel in the Collaborative Process

The development of full-service schools almost always involves the organization of representatives from different agencies into interagency teams that come together to provide students with a continuum of services in a way that requires delineation of structural connections between providers, mechanisms for the exchange of information, and procedures that facilitate cooperation (Adelman & Taylor, 1993, 1997b, 1998, 1999; Noblit & Cobb, 1997). Noblit and Cobb described two important dimensions of this collaborative process: (a) factors that promote versus discourage decisions to collaborate (spurs vs. reins) and (b) things that make collaboration less versus more difficult (grease vs. gravel). As competition for funding has increased among human service organizations, fiscal issues are often the most significant spur promoting decisions to cooperate. Unfortunately, once agreements to work together are reached, there may be more gravel than grease as the collaborative process unfolds.

Under the best of circumstances, interagency programs are difficult to create, and collaboration can be threatened by both problems specific to the process itself and preexisting problems that organizations bring to the process (Adelman & Taylor, 1997b; Crowson & Boyd, 1993). Therefore, when building interagency collaboratives, local planning groups should be aware that lack of stable leadership, fiscal problems, poor administration, and staff turnover within organizations can affect their ability to contribute as expected. As the planning process unfolds and stakeholders express interest in participating, the work group must establish mechanisms to evaluate the potential for each organization to contribute as expected, specify ways potential threats to effective participation will be addressed, and monitor the implementation of changes to support ongoing participation.

Once the players have come together, collaboration can also be contaminated by different levels of expertise and different levels of commitment among the staff expected to contribute on a day-to-day basis. As collaboratives form, staff from some organizations may come with the desired skills but only limited commitment to innovative service delivery; others may come enthusiastic about the concept of school-based service delivery but without the professional skills needed to work effectively with the target population. Again, local planning groups will need mechanisms to determine whether the staff being considered for certain roles have the requisite skills and general commitment needed to make a valuable contribution to an interagency team. More important, as projects begin, interagency collaboratives will also need mechanisms to ensure that, once chosen, staff receive the training they need to work effectively with the target population in a manner that supports integrated service delivery (for a discussion, see Short, 1997).

Once underway, the collaborative process can be jeopardized by an array of other potential problems. For example, beneath facades of agreement about a common vision hammered out over time, different parties may privately maintain different visions of the same program. Likewise, even in the midst of agreement about the importance of all services and the need for innovative approaches to service delivery, the universal tendency to defend professional turf and adhere to traditional modes of operating can undermine the development of interagency teams as professionals from different disciplines struggle about the relative value of who does what and how it gets done (Flaherty et al., 1998; Noblit & Cobb, 1997; Waxman, Weist, & Benson, 1999). Perhaps even more so than in other professional work environments, economic, ethnic, gender, personality, and lifestyle differences can also generate difficulty as project staff are assembled (Adelman & Taylor, 1997b; Noblit & Cobb, 1997). Finally, intervention teams that span agencies can also create divided loyalty among staff who must balance their commitment to the collaborative against their commitment to their home agency (Crowson & Boyd, 1993).

That said, problems associated with turf, communication, allocation of resources, and bureaucracy tend to quickly resolve when planning groups seriously consider fundamental questions about organizational structure and the dynamics of collaboration. As Crowson and Boyd (1993) suggested, formal documentation of goals, clear delineation of expectations, contracts that stipulate the nature of interagency relationships, diagrams specifying organizational structure, and outlines of policies and procedures usually help promote collaboration. Group process that leaves participants feeling involved in equitable, productive, reciprocal relationships that represent a new organization with its own identity also helps tremendously (Adelman & Taylor, 1997b).

Team process that focuses on the needs of the school and the development of the service delivery system, rather than the needs of individual students, can also promote interagency collaboration (Adelman & Taylor, 1998, 1999; Waxman et al., 1999). Sharing resources and work space may also help (Crowson & Boyd, 1993). More than anything else, 3 to 5 years of time working together may be necessary for interagency collaboratives to congeal (Annie E. Casey Foundation, 1995; Dryfoos, 1998; Waxman et al., 1999). Regardless of what else gets done to promote collaboration, interested parties must come together around a shared goal; be willing to participate in something that will evolve over years; and become comfortable enough with one another to share ideas, disagree, resolve differences, and build commitment to pursue the original vision.

Moving Services into the Schools: Building Community–School Relationships

Inevitably, moving service delivery teams into schools will raise questions about how to work with school staff. When beginning, planning groups must pay close attention to the attitudes and perceptions of all school staff and make deliberate efforts to build positive, yet very different, working relationships with school principals, classroom teachers, and pupil personnel professionals. Although the local school board, superintendent of schools, and central administration must approve projects and support implementation from afar, the success of any school-based collaborative will hinge on the school principal taking a leadership stance that facilitates implementation (Jehl & Kirst, 1992). To succeed, collaboratives must establish positive working relationships with school principals in the best position to negotiate with political factions within the school organization; mediate differences of opinion; forge alliances; and shape a less competitive, more cooperative school climate (Crowson & Boyd, 1993).

Moving services into the schools will also raise questions about how to directly involve classroom teachers as more than just referral agents. As with school principals, the success of any school-based project will depends on the support of classroom teachers who are accustomed to working in relative isolation with a great deal of autonomy (Crowson & Boyd, 1993). Although there has been little discussion about the role that classroom teachers might play in the development of these initiatives, new collaboratives must include teachers in the planning process, define expectations for them, and ensure that they remain involved during all phases of implementation.

Similarly, several authors (e.g., Adelman, 1996; Adelman & Taylor, 1997a, 1998, 1999) have highlighted the need to include pupil personnel staff who, more so than any other group, may feel threatened by the presence of community collaboratives. As full-service schools have become more common, professionals across disciplines (e.g., Adelman & Taylor, 1998; Reeder et al., 1997; Waxman et al., 1999) have begun to define clear roles for pupil personnel staff and to closely examine the point at which school staff interfaces with community providers. Moreover, Adelman and Taylor (1998, 1999) argued that the analysis of existing resources and the integration of community and pupil personnel resources into a single unit is a necessary, but typically missing, step in the organization of this type of collaborative.

As the concept of full-service schools evolves, meaningful roles for parents also need to be better defined (Bickham, Pizarro, Warner, Rosenthal, & Weist, 1998). Again, parent participation is one of those simple ideas that is easy to embrace but difficult to define and promote. Under some circumstances, it may be very difficult to mobilize parents, particularly in settings where school staff have historically not valued parent participation or in settings where, for other reasons, parents have felt alienated from school institutions. School reform movements (e.g., see Haynes & Comer, 1996) have consistently outlined strategies to promote parent participation in the reorganization of schools, and local planning groups should begin the process aware that creative, persistent efforts to promote parent participation may be needed over an extended period of time (for a discussion, see Bickham et al., 1998). With recognition that parental involvement in schooling is a complex, multidetermined phenomenon (Smith, Connell, Wright, Sizer, & Norman, 1997), it is important to note that parents living in high-risk environments often come to school when goods and services that meet their basic needs are available within the school building (Crowson & Boyd, 1993).

Putting It Together: Parallel Versus Integrated Structures

Moving service delivery teams into school buildings will also raise questions about the ways school environments must change to accommodate collaboration (Crowson & Boyd, 1993). Inevitably, collaborative efforts will provoke innumerable questions about power, authority, mission, boundaries, and protocols for working with educators, students, and parents. Given that the primary goal remains the education of students, full-service schools must balance the educational needs of students against their need for support services. Concretely, this dilemma often gets translated into difficult questions about when and how services are delivered, particularly if projects follow the advice of Adelman (1996; Adelman & Taylor, 1998, 1999) and work to establish the enabling component as an equal partner in the educational process. Simply put, when students need to learn at the same time they need support services to address issues interfering with learning, how do structures and protocols for working together ensure that students receive both?

The concept of full-services schools embraces not just change in service delivery, but also change in the quality of education children receive (Dryfoos, 1994a, 1998; Holtzman, 1992, 1997). As partnerships think about more effective, innovative approaches to instruction, questions about the role the enabling component should play in the development of the instructional component will undoubtedly emerge. Although everyone involved may believe school staff reserve the right to help shape service delivery, partnerships may find themselves struggling with questions about whether service-delivery staff should be helping to shape the instructional process. In settings where instructional staff neither expect, nor welcome input from support staff, the questions may only be asked within the enabling component. The issue can also become much more pointed if, over time, staff within the enabling component become concerned about the adequacy of the educational experience children are receiving. The issue is that, for whatever reasons, instructional staff may be very comfortable addressing questions about the quality of support services, but support staff may be very reluctant to address questions about the quality of the educational experience. As collaboration unfolds, planning groups must develop mechanisms to ensure communication about the quality of both across components.

Professionals building full-service schools must also acknowledge that this dynamic tends to occur, at least in part, because in most projects, school systems retain a disproportionate share of the power and authority. Services are only located in school buildings with formal approval of the local school board and the administrative hierarchy. Critics (e.g., Gardner, 1992; Chaskin & Richman, 1992) sensitive to the power differential have argued that, regardless of the initial agreement, there is always danger that, once operational, school-based collaboratives may be co-opted by school personnel, and initial goals may be displaced as service delivery begins to be shaped by the needs of the school system rather than the needs of the students.

Consequently, as collaborations evolve and enabling components receive inappropriate requests for assistance or requests to somehow alter parameters that were defined as the project began, they must recognize that complying might help promote good will, but complying might also be the first step in a process that begins moving the project in a direction people may not want to go. Tactful refusal of requests to help in ways not originally agreed upon may actually help build more appropriate relationships over the long term. As Gardner (1992) cautioned, if some effort is not made to preserve the original vision, school-based collaboratives can quickly become nothing more than another layer of ineffective bureaucracy that becomes focused on fixing problems within children rather than addressing problems, including systemic problems, affecting children.

Within the literature on the development of full-service schools, several authors (e.g., Adelman & Taylor, 1997a, 1999; Crowson & Boyd, 1993; Dryfoos, 1994a; Jehl & Kirst, 1992) have also highlighted the need for new governance structures that redistribute power and authority within school organizations. Partnership agreements for the creation of full-service schools currently do not, for the most part, change the status quo by establishing wholly new structures (Adelman & Taylor, 1997a, 1999; Dryfoos, 1994a, 1995). Instead, they tend to simply specify how services will be integrated into an existing school setting. Usually, two separate administrative structures co-exist, sometimes under the watchful eye of a coordinating committee that includes representation of key stakeholders from both sides of the fence.

Regardless of the initial goals, this type of structure typically leads to the creation of parallel instructional and enabling components without true integration (Adelman & Taylor, 1997a, 1999). As the concept evolves, some observers (e.g., Adelman, 1996) have argued that the real challenge is to develop innovative governance structures that redistribute power and authority within the school so that community providers become more than a guest in a school owned and run by someone else. If fortunate enough to be at that point in the process, local planning groups will want to closely examine evolving structures in the educational reform movement that support decentralization of decision making and shared responsibility for the creation of truly unique school environments (for a review, see Dryfoos, 1998).

Linking Access with School Attendance: What If We Build It and No One Comes?

Although often not stated explicitly, full-service schools link access to services with school attendance. Their success depends on the assumption that, if nothing else, youth living in high-risk environments will come to a school building. From the beginning, it is important to note that this assumption is at odds with overwhelming evidence that students at greatest risk are more likely to be truant and less likely to remain enrolled through high school graduation. Given this, moving services to schools may actually limit, rather than expand, access for the group most in need because that group may simply not be in school. Although proponents of full-service schools have offered a rationale for locating services in school buildings, others (e.g., Chaskin & Richman, 1992; Romualdi & Sandoval, 1997) have argued that decisions to locate services in school buildings may actually hamper service delivery.

Accordingly, when schools do not serve a specific neighborhood, the initiative intends to target teens that are less likely to be in school, or specific circumstances complicate plans to move a program into schools, local planning groups should seriously consider locating the program at another site and inviting the school system to make educational services available there. In her accounting of programs being developed across the country, Dryfoos (1998) described several projects that began as community-based initiatives and then added educational services in an effort to create comprehensive service centers for youth. Again, our intent is not to discourage the development of school-based collaboratives, but rather to highlight the idea that there are equally viable conceptual models grounded in a community, rather than a school, perspective on service delivery that may need to be seriously examined as the process begins (for a discussion, see Romualdi & Sandoval, 1997).

Moreover, if after careful deliberation local planning groups decide to move programming into schools, they must proceed with awareness that practical issues about the relation between school attendance and access to support services will emerge immediately. Must students be enrolled at a specific school to receive services there? What happens to the enabling component in those jurisdictions where school closes during the summer months? How do intervention teams engage those students who are most alienated from the educational process and most wary about turning to anyone in a school building for assistance? Can medically ill, psychiatrically disturbed, truant, or suspended students be in the building to receive support services during school hours? What happens when a student receiving services is expelled? What happens when a student who graduates wants to continue receiving support services, particularly when there have been positive, long-term relationships with service providers? How will the collaborative reach out to truant students and students who have withdrawn from school? Again, the goal here is to simply highlight the fact that *school-based* typically means *attendance-linked* so that local planning groups can plan accordingly.

Legal, Ethical, and Professional Considerations

Moving services to school buildings for delivery by an interagency collaborative tends to also generate a host of legal and ethical questions about informed consent, confidentiality, and professional responsibility. For example, who should provide consent for services, and how should permission be secured, especially when the program will serve teens who may have the psychological capacity to provide informed consent but not the legal authority to do so? Are open consents obtained from parents at the beginning of the school year adequate from a legal and ethical perspective, or should more specific consent be obtained every time a student seeks a new service? How will programs deal with different guidelines concerning age of legal consent for different types of services? Is consent necessary for programming provided to all students attending the school as part of their educational curriculum?

Similarly, do members of interagency teams located in the same school building need written permission to communicate with one another about students who are receiving services? What information should be communicated to school staff, under what circumstances, and with permission from whom? Who retains responsibility for the management of crises involving suicidal, intoxicated, assaultive, or acutely ill students? What liability do licensed professionals incur if they are on grounds and choose not to assist with the management of a crisis or if they are not asked to do so? What happens when licensed mental health professionals are asked to assist in determining whether potentially suicidal or assaultive students should be in school?

Moving services to schools may also create ethical dilemmas for providers involving their role within the school organization. For example, what happens when school-based providers learn school staff are violating student rights, standing policy, or administrative directives? What responsibility do school-based providers have to enforce rules about student behavior on school grounds? Should school-based providers be thinking of themselves as advocates for students within the educational system (for a discussion, see McMahon, 1993)? How do collaboratives accommodate the ethical standards of different professions who come together to provide services in a coordinated manner? Under what circumstances do collaboratives end unproductive relationships with school systems (for a discussion, see McMahon & Pruett, 1998)? The lesson here is the idea that complex legal and ethical issues will always emerge, and projects will need access to legal consultation and formal mechanisms to support examination and resolution of important ethical questions.

When building community-school collaboratives, local planning groups will also be forced to consider important questions about the focus of the services offered. The concept of full-service schools emphasizes the development of a full continuum of services ranging from preventive to remedial (Adelman & Taylor, 1993, 1998, 1999; Chaskin & Richman, 1992). That said, when resources are limited, and a full continuum of services is needed, especially as programs are first being organized, how do local planning teams decide which services get offered sooner rather than later? This question may be further complicated by the service demands of students and parents who tend to be crisis oriented. When the demand for crisis intervention and clinical services for acute problems is greatest, how do flexible resources get distributed so that preventive services and early intervention also get developed? Although conceptual models that outline a full continuum must remain the ideal that serves as the basis for program development, local planning groups must begin the process aware that finances, the demands of the target population, preferences of school staff, and other practical problems may make it difficult to develop and maintain the balanced continuum of services outlined by Adelman and Taylor (1993, 1998, 1999).

Process and Outcome Evaluation: Please Just Prove It Works

Organizations that fund innovative service delivery systems almost always demand some evaluation of implementation, effectiveness, and potential for replication in other settings. However, despite reported interest in documenting implementation and effectiveness, there are a number of persistent issues that tend to complicate the evaluation of full-service schools. Although everyone (e.g., Illback et al., 1997) emphasizes the importance of both process and outcome evlauation, funding sources seem, in the current climate of accountability, to be more and more interested in outcomes. Few funding sources acknowledge that the efficacy of an intervention can only be demonstrated after the prototype has been fully implemented and operational for several years (Adelman & Taylor, 1997b; Crowson & Boyd, 1993; Dryfoos, 1998). Funding agencies typically support demonstration projects with an expectation that, after a brief period of implementation, programs should be able to document immediate change in targeted outcomes. Recipients are often more interested in program development over time and the longer-term impact. Inevitably, evaluation teams seem to repeatedly end up pursuing mandates to prove it works before being able to prove it has been fully and properly implemented. Ironically, as Adelman and Taylor (1997b) pointed out, what is currently needed most in this climate of increased accountability is good data about implementation.

In addition to being pursued prematurely and often to the exclusion of good process evaluation, the evaluative process can be plagued by a host of other problems specific to the nature of outcome evaluations. Historically, there has been a bias that defines qualitative methods as most appropriate for process evaluation and quantitative methods as most appropriate for outcome evaluation. There has been an emphasis on *variable-based* approaches to data analysis pursued in an effort to document global change in outcomes within an entire school rather than an emphasis on the use of *individual-based* approaches (for a description, see Bergman & Magnusson, 1997) that might more readily document the change within subgroups of students that most observers (e.g., Dryfoos, 1998) expect to occur. Similarly, the emphasis on quantitative methods has contributed to ongoing enthusiasm about research paradigms that are not practical for use in schools. Proponents (e.g., Gomby & Larson, 1992) of rigorous evaluation advocate the use of experimental methods that are typically used in controlled clinical trials conducted in medical settings, but this methodology does not generalize well to school settings, where random assignment of individuals is rarely possible; appropriate comparison groups often do not exist; comprehensive measurement of behavioral outcomes is difficult; and longitudinal follow-up can be both difficult and expensive, particularly if a cohort of students being followed moves on to other school programs or leaves the system (Illback et al., 1997).

In addition, just as there are questions about who pays for the development of programming, there are even more difficult questions about who pays for the comprehensive evaluation everyone calls for. Demonstration grants often allow for program evaluation, but they typically limit funding that can be devoted to evaluation, while they simultaneously set forth expectations for a comprehensive evaluation that can rarely be done with the budget allowed. State and local funding for service delivery, coordination, and integration rarely includes provisions for program evaluation. Funding specifically for program evaluation may be available from federal agencies or private foundations, but that income may not be available on the same timetable as funding being used to support implementation of the program. As funding streams present unrealistic expectations about evaluation, local planning groups need, as much as possible, to temper those expectations by arguing for reasonable, creative, cost-efficient approaches to process and outcome evaluation that will provide potentially useful data about implementation and effectiveness.

CONCLUSIONS

As awareness that school systems alone cannot, and should not, be expected to address the social problems affecting the education of millions of children, the concept of full-service schools has been presented as a potential solution to many of the service delivery problems affecting children who are living in high-risk situations. Across the country, hundreds of initiatives are being pursued within a broad conceptual framework defined primarily by a common perspective on child development and commitment to a specific strategy for more effective delivery of human services. As the full-service school movement evolves, critical roles for consultants with different types of expertise will continue to emerge as local planning groups seek assistance with the organization, implementation, and maintenance of new initiatives.

Clearly, as psychological and educational consultants join local planning groups to help build full-service schools, they must do so with awareness of existing projects and factors known to facilitate collaboration. However, as they journey into this particular world of systems reform, they must also be prepared to look beyond simple examination of successful projects and carefully consider factors that have hampered program development, so that they will be in a position to help planning groups deal in an effective, proactive manner with some of the obstacles that will inevitably complicate implementation. Moreover, as consultants work diligently to promote the development of effective collaboratives, they must look to expand their working knowledge of factors undermining implementation so that, as the next millennium begins, they will be in a position to help local working groups develop interagency collaboratives that more effectively integrate school and human service systems, increase service use, and promote positive developmental outcomes for children living in high-risk situations.

ACKNOWLEDGMENT

This work was supported by the U.S. Department of Education, Safe and Drug-Free Schools Program (Grant S184 D60214), the Connecticut Department of Mental Health and Addiction Services, and the New Haven Public School System.

REFERENCES

Adelman, H. S. (1993). School-linked mental health interventions: Toward mechanism for service coordination and integration. *Journal of Community Psychology, 21,* 309–319.

Adelman, H. S. (1996). Restructuring education support services and integrating community resources: Beyond the full service school model. *School Psychology Review, 25,* 431– 445.

Adelman, H. S., & Taylor, L. (1993). School-based mental health: Toward a comprehensive approach. *Journal of Mental Health Administration, 20,* 32–45.

Adelman, H. S., & Taylor, L. (1997a). Addressing barriers to learning: Beyond school-linked services and full-service schools. *American Journal of Orthopsychiatry, 67,* 408–421.

Adelman, H. S., & Taylor, L. (1997b). Toward a scale-up model for replicating new approaches to schooling. *Journal of Educational and Psychological Consultation, 8,* 197–230.

Adelman, H. S., & Taylor, L. (1998). Mental health in schools. *School Psychology Review, 27,* 175–190.

Adelman, H. S., & Taylor, L. (1999). Mental health in schools and system restructuring. *Clinical Psychology Review, 19,* 137–163.

Adelman, H. S., Barker, L. A., & Nelson, P. (1993). A study of a school-based clinic: Who uses it and who doesn't? *Journal of Clinical Child Psychology, 22,* 52–59.

Adelman, H. S., Taylor, L., Weist, M. D., Adelsheim, S., Freeman, B., Kapp, L., Lahti, M., & Mawn, D. (1999). Mental health in schools: A federal initiative. *Children's Services: Social Policy, Research, and Practice, 2,* 95–115.

Allensworth, D. D., Lawson, E. L., Nicholson, L., & Wyche, J. H. (Eds.). (1997). *Schools and health: Our nation's investment.* Washington, DC: National Academy Press.

Annie E. Casey Foundation. (1995). *The path of most resistance: Reflections on lessons learned from New Futures, 1995.* Baltimore, MD: Author.

Armbruster, P., Andrews, E., Couenhoven, J., & Blau, G. (1999). Collusion or collaboration? School-based services meet managed care. *Clinical Psychology Review, 19,* 221– 227.

Bergman, L. R., & Magnusson, D. (1997). A person-oriented approach in research on developmental psychopathology. *Development and Psychopathology, 9,* 291–319.

Bickman, L. (1996). A continuum of care: More is not always better. *American Psychologist, 51,* 689–701.

Bickham, N. L., Pizarro, L. J., Warner, B. S., Rosenthal, B., & Weist, M. D. (1998). Family involvement in expanded school mental health. *Journal of School Health, 68,* 425–428.

Calfee, C., Wittwer, F., & Meredith, M. (1998). *Building a full-service school: A step-by- step guide.* San Francisco: Jossey-Bass.

Carlson, C. I., Paavola, J. C., & Talley, R. C. (1995). Historical, current, and future models of schools as health care delivery settings. *School Psychology Quarterly, 10,* 184–202.

Carlson, C. I., Tharinger, D. J., Bricklin, P. M., DeMers, S. T., & Paavola, J. C. (1996). Health care reform and psychological practice in schools. *Professional Psychology: Research and Practice, 27,* 14–23.

Chaskin, R. J., & Richman, H. A. (1992). Concerns about school-linked services: Institution-based versus community-based models. *The Future of Children, 2,* 107–117.

Cowen, E. L., Hightower, A. D., Pedro-Caroll, J. L., Work, W. C., Wyman, P. A., & Haffey, W. G. (1996). *School-based prevention for children at risk: The Primary Mental Health Program.* Washington, DC: American Psychological Association.

Cross, T. P., & Saxe, L. (1997). Many hands make mental health systems of care a reality: Lessons for the Mental Health Services Program for Youth. In C. T. Nixon & D. A. Northrup (Eds.), *Evaluating mental health services: How do programs for children work in the real world* (pp. 45–72). Thousand Oaks, CA: Sage.

Crowson, R. L., & Boyd, W. L. (1993). Coordinated services for children: Designing arks for storms and seas unknown. *American Journal of Education, 101,* 140–179.

Davidson, L., Pruett, M. K., McMahon, T. J., Ward, N. L., & Griffith, E. E. (in press). Comprehensive interventions for at-risk urban youth: Applying lessons from the community mental health movement. *Children's Services: Social Policy, Research, and Practice.*

Dryfoos, J. G. (1994a). *Full-service schools: A revolution in health and social services for children, youth, and families.* San Francisco: Jossey-Bass.

Dryfoos, J. G. (1994b). Medical clinics in junior high school: Changing the model to meet demands. *Journal of Adolescent Health, 15,* 549–557.

Dryfoos, J. G. (1995). Full service schools: Revolution or fad? *Journal of Research on Adolescence, 5,* 147–172.

Dryfoos, J. G. (1997). School-based youth programs: Exemplary models and emerging opportunities. In R. J. Illback, C. T. Cobb, & H. M. Joseph (Eds.), *Integrated services for children and families: Opportunities for psychological practice* (pp. 23–52). Washington, DC: American Psychological Association.

Dryfoos, J. G. (1998). *Safe passage: Making it through adolescence in a risky society.* New York: Oxford University Press.

Eber, L., & Nelson, C. M. (1997). School-based wraparound planning: Integrating services for students with emotional and behavioral needs. *American Journal of Orthopsychiatry, 67,* 385–395.

Fagan, T. K. (1985). Sources for the delivery of school psychological services during 1890-1930. *School Psychology Review, 14,* 378–382.

Fagan, T. K. (1987a). Gesell: The first school psychologist. Part I: The road to Connecticut. *School Psychology Review, 16,* 103–107.

Fagan, T. K. (1987b). Gesell: The first school psychologist. Part II: Practice and significance. *School Psychology Review, 16,* 399–409.

Fagan, T. K. (1996). Witmer's contributions to school psychological services. *American Psychologist, 51,* 241–243.

Farrow, F., & Joe, T. (1992). Financing school-linked, integrated services. *The Future of Children, 2,* 56–67.

Finn-Stevenson, M. (1992). Paving the way: Questions and criteria for the School of the Future. In W. H. Holtzman (Ed.), *School of the future* (pp. 45–59). Washington, DC: American Psychological Association & Hogg Foundation for Mental Health.

Flaherty, L. T., Garrison, E. G., Waxman, R., Uris, P. F., Keys, S. G., Glass-Siegal, M., & Weist, M. D. (1998). Optimizing the roles of school mental health professionals. *Journal of School Health, 68,* 420–424.

Flaherty, L. T., Weist, M. D., & Warner, B. S. (1996). School-based mental health services in the United States: History, current models, and needs. *Community Mental Health Journal, 32,* 341–352.

Gardner, S. L. (1992). Key issues in developing school-linked, integrated services. *The Future of Children, 2,* 85–94.

Garrison, E. G., Roy, I. S., & Azar, V. (1999). Responding to the mental health needs of Latino children and families through school-based services. *Clinical Psychology Review, 19,* 199–219.

Gomby, D. S., & Larson, C. S. (1992). Evaluation of school-linked services. *The Future of Children, 2,* 68–84.

Hawkins, J. W., Hayes, E. R., & Corliss, C. P. (1994). School nursing in America. *Public Health Nursing, 11,* 416–425.

Haynes, N. M., & Comer, J. P. (1996). Integrating schools, families, and communities through successful school reform: The School Development Program. *School Psychology Review, 25,* 501–506.

Holtzman, W. H. (1992). Community renewal, family preservation, and child development through the School of the Future. In W. H. Holtzman (Ed.), *School of the future* (pp. 3–18). Washington, DC: American Psychological Association & Hogg Foundation for Mental Health.

Holtzman, W. H. (1997). Community psychology and full-service schools in different cultures. *American Psychologist, 52,* 381–389.

Illback, R. J., Kalafat, J., & Sanders, D. (1997). Evaluating integrated service programs. In R. J. Illback, C. T. Cobb, & H. M. Joseph (Eds.), *Integrated services for children and families: Opportunities for psychological practice* (pp. 323–346). Washington, DC: American Psychological Association.

Jehl, J., & Kirst, M. (1992). Getting ready to provide school-linked services: What schools must do. *The Future of Children, 2,* 96–106.

Kolbe, L. J., Collins, J., & Cortese, P. (1997). Building the capacity of schools to improve the health of the nation: A call for assistance for psychologists. *American Psychologist, 52,* 256–265.

Larson, C. S., Gomby, D. S., Shiono, P. H., Lewit, E. M., & Behrman, R. E. (1992). School-linked services: Analysis. *The Future of Children, 2,* 6–18.

Levy, J. E., & Shepardson, W. (1992). A look at current school-linked service efforts. *The Future of Children, 2,* 44–55.

McMahon, T. J. (1993). On the concept of child advocacy: A review of theory and methodology. *School Psychology Review, 22,* 744–755.

McMahon, T. J., & Pruett, M. K. (1998). On the proverbial horns of an ethical dilemma: School consultation, child advocacy, and adversarial intervention. *Journal of Educational and Psychological Consultation, 9,* 75–85.

Melton, G. B. (1997). Why don't the knuckleheads use common sense? In S. W. Henggeler & A. B. Santos (Eds.), *Innovative approaches for difficult-to-treat populations* (pp. 351–370). Washington, DC: American Psychiatric Press.

Morrill, W. A. (1992). Overview of service delivery to children. *The Future of Children, 2,* 32–43.

Noblit, G. W., & Cobb, C. T. (1997). Organizing for effective integrated services. In R. J. Illback, C. T. Cobb, & H. M. Joseph (Eds.), *Integrated services for children and families: Opportunities for psychological practice* (pp. 191–220). Washington, DC: American Psychological Association.

Orland, M. E., Danegger, A. E., & Foley, E. (1997). The critical role of finance in creating comprehensive support systems. In R. J. Illback, C. T. Cobb, & H. M. Joseph (Eds.), *Integrated services for children and families: Opportunities for psychological practice* (pp. 93–118). Washington, DC: American Psychological Association.

Paavola, J. C., Carey, K., Cobb, C., Illback, R. J., Joseph, H. M., Routh, D. K., & Torruella, A. (1996). Interdisciplinary school practice: Implications of the service integration movement for psychologists. *Professional Psychology: Research and Practice, 27,* 34–40.

Paavola, J. C., Hannah, F. P., & Nichol, G. T. (1989). The Memphis City Schools Mental Health Center: A program description. *Professional School Psychology, 4,* 61–74.

Phillips, V., Boysen, T. C., & Schuster, S. A. (1997). Psychology's role in statewide education reform: Kentucky as an example. *American Psychologist, 52,* 250–255.

Reeder, G. D., Maccow, G. C., Shaw, S. R., Swerdlik, M. E., Horton, C. B., & Foster, P. (1997). School psychologists and full-service schools: Partnerships with medical, mental health, and social services. *School Psychology Review, 26,* 603–621.

Romualdi, V., & Sandoval, J. (1997). Community-based service integration: Family resource center initiatives. In R. J. Illback, C. T. Cobb, & H. M. Joseph (Eds.), *Integrated services for children and families: Opportunities for psychological practice* (pp. 53–73). Washington, DC: American Psychological Association.

Sedlak, M. W. (1997). The uneasy alliance of mental health services and the schools: An historical perspective. *American Journal of Orthopsychiatry, 67,* 349–362.

Short, R. J. (1997). Education and training for integrated practice: Assumptions, components, and issues. In R. J. Illback, C. T. Cobb, & H. M. Joseph (Eds.), *Integrated services for children and families: Opportunities for psychological practice* (pp. 347–357). Washington, DC: American Psychological Association.

Short, R. J., & Talley, R. C. (1997). Rethinking psychology and the schools: Implications of recent national policy. *American Psychologist, 52,* 234–240.

Smith, E. P., Connell, C. M., Wright, G., Sizer, M., & Norman, J. M. (1997). An ecological model of home, school, and community partnerships: Implications for research and practice. *Journal of Educational and Psychological Consultation, 8,* 339–360.

Talley, R. C., & Short, R. J. (1996). Social reforms and the future of school practice: Implications for American psychology. *Professional Psychology: Research and Practice, 27,* 5–13.

Tyack, D. (1992). Health and social services in public schools: A historical perspective. *The Future of Children, 2,* 19–31.

Waxman, R. P., Weist, M. D., & Benson, D. M. (1999). Toward collaboration in the growing education-mental health interface. *Clinical Psychology Review, 19,* 239–253.

Weist, M. D. (1997). Expanded school mental health services: A national movement in progress. In T. H. Ollendick & R. J. Prinz (Eds.), *Advances in clinical child psychology* (pp. 319–352). New York: Plenum Press.

Zigler, E. F., Finn-Stevenson, M., & Stern, B. M. (1997). Supporting children and families in the schools: The School of the 21st Century. *American Journal of Orthopsychiatry, 67,* 396–407.

Thomas J. McMahon is an Assistant Professor in the Department of Psychiatry and Child Study Center at the Yale University School of Medicine, and he is Director of a satellite clinic of the Connecticut Mental Health Center. Dr. McMahon is interested in clinical–school collaboration and the development of community-based mental health services for children, particularly children affected by parental substance abuse.

Nadia L. Ward is an Associate Research Scientist in the Department of Psychiatry at the Yale University School of Medicine, and she is Program Coordinator for a full-service alternative high school. Dr. Ward is interested in the psychosocial development of ethnic minority youth and the design of preventive interventions for teens living in inner-city environments.

Marsha Kline Pruett is a Research Scientist in the Departments of Psychiatry and Child Study Center at the Yale University School of Medicine, and she is Director of Child And Adolescent Programs at The Consultation Center. Dr. Kline is interested in the legal and ethical dimensions of consultation and the development of interventions designed to promote social and emotional competence in children facing school and family transitions.

Larry Davidson is an Associate Professor in the Department of Psychiatry at the Yale University School of Medicine, and he is Director of Clinical Services at the Connecticut Mental Health Center. Dr. Davidson is interested in the development of community-based systems of mental health services and community integration of individuals with serious, persistent psychiatric disorders.

Ezra E. H. Griffith is a Professor of Psychiatry and African American Studies and Deputy Chair for Clinical Affairs in the Department of Psychiatry at the Yale University School of Medicine. Dr. Griffith is interested in cross-cultural issues in psychiatry, transracial adoption, and the administration of mental health services in the public sector.

JOURNAL OF EDUCATIONAL AND PSYCHOLOGICAL CONSULTATION, *11*(1), 93–120

You *Can* Get There From Here: Using a Theory of Change Approach to Plan Urban Education Reform

James P. Connell and Adena M. Klem

The Institute for Research and Reform in Education

This article presents a theory of change approach to *planning* educational reform initiatives with a focus on district level efforts. Using examples from ongoing consulting work with urban school districts, we walk through steps in a planning process that can yield a theory of change that meets 4 criteria: plausible, doable, testable, and meaningful. The benefits of this planning approach for evaluation and implementation of district level educational reform are also discussed. We conclude with implications of this approach for educational and psychological consultants working with educational reform initiatives.

Every urban school district in America has had some form of district-wide reform plan, and most have had multiple plans over the past decade. In light of this extraordinary effort by many talented people, why do we not see more examples of meaningful, district-wide improvement in student performance? First and foremost, because it is really hard to do. The inherent complexity of system change, the cyclical nature of public attention to urban education, and the divisive factors of race and class that plague local and national consideration of urban issues make planning and implementing meaningful change in urban schools an awesome challenge.

In our work as consultants to urban education reform initiatives, we have found the "theory of change" approach[1] (Connell & Kubisch, 1998) to

---

Correspondence should be addressed to James P. Connell, Institute for Research and Reform in Education, 710 Glengarry Road, Philadelphia, PA 19118.

[1] The description and rationale of the approach draws on our earlier work (Connell & Klem, 1996), and shares some key elements with other planning and evaluation approaches as well.

planning these initiatives helpful in three ways. The approach helps make plans for urban education more sensible—more grounded in current research, in demonstrated best practice, and in local experience. It builds a local knowledge base and collective change ethic that makes implementation of the reform more likely. And, finally, this approach makes evaluation of these plans more rigorous, timely, and useful.

This article describes the theory of change approach to planning educational reform. It is organized into three sections: (a) an overview of the approach as it is being applied to planning complex community-based initiatives; (b) the steps involved in a theory of change planning process and examples of its products; and (c) a summary of this approach's challenges, benefits, and implications for educational and psychological consultants working in diverse educational settings. Throughout this article, our ongoing work in one urban school district[2] is used as a case example to illustrate how the approach works.

OVERVIEW OF THE THEORY OF CHANGE APPROACH

Just what is a *theory of change*? Weiss (1995) defines it quite simply as a theory of how and why an initiative works. According to Connell and Kubisch (1998), the approach has several key elements, some of which are shared with other planning approaches (Argyris, 1993; Argyris & Schon, 1974; Fetterman, Kaftarian, & Wandersman, 1995; Hustedde & Score, 1995; Julian, Jones, & Deyo, 1995; Kaufman & Herman, 1991).

First, a theory of change delineates the pathway of an initiative by making explicit both the outcomes of an initiative (early, intermediate, and longer term) and the action strategies that will lead to the achievement of these outcomes. Second, the quality of a theory of change is judged by four explicit criteria: how plausible, doable, testable, and meaningful the theory of change is.

> *Plausible* means that stakeholders believe the logic of the model is correct: if we do these things, we will get the results we want and expect.

---

[2]This is a small, urban district with approximately 23,000 students, over 60% of which are minority; 80% are eligible for public support of some kind. Approximately 40% of incoming freshman do not graduate from high school. In our 3 years of work with the district, there have been three superintendents, redistricting because of desegregation, and three board elections.

Doable means the human, political, and economic resources are seen as sufficient to implement the action strategies in the theory.

Testable means that stakeholders believe there are credible ways to discover whether the results are as predicted.

Meaningful means that stakeholders see the outcomes as important and see the magnitude of change in these outcomes being pursued as worth the effort.

Third, a theory of change is generated by "moving backward" from long-term goals and outcomes to the necessary and sufficient conditions (intermediate and early outcomes) for producing those long-term outcomes to action strategies needed to achieve early outcomes (see Figure 1). Fourth, this approach considers not only whether change will occur, but also how much change is expected to occur, for what populations, and in what settings and when. Fifth, it examines expectations for outcomes and activities in light of available and potential resources. Sixth, the approach encourages multiple stakeholders to contribute to articulation of the theory of change. And, seventh, the approach recognizes that the theory of change can change as it is tested over the course of the initiative.

Next, we walk through the steps in applying this approach by using a case example from our own work.

BUILDING A "GOOD" THEORY OF CHANGE

Step 1: Generate or Adopt an Initial Change Framework

The planning process begins by importing an initial change framework, such as the one shown in Figure 2, which was developed by the Institute for Research and Reform in Education (IRRE) for use in a project involving three urban school districts, a national technical assistance provider, and a private national funder. IRRE's role was to design a process whereby these three urban districts could place the funder's investment in an overarching theory of change to guide their ongoing and future reform efforts. This par-

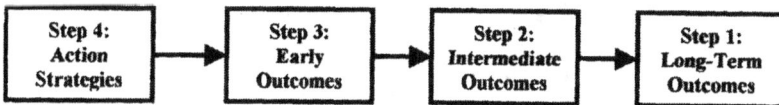

FIGURE 1   Steps in articulating a theory of change.

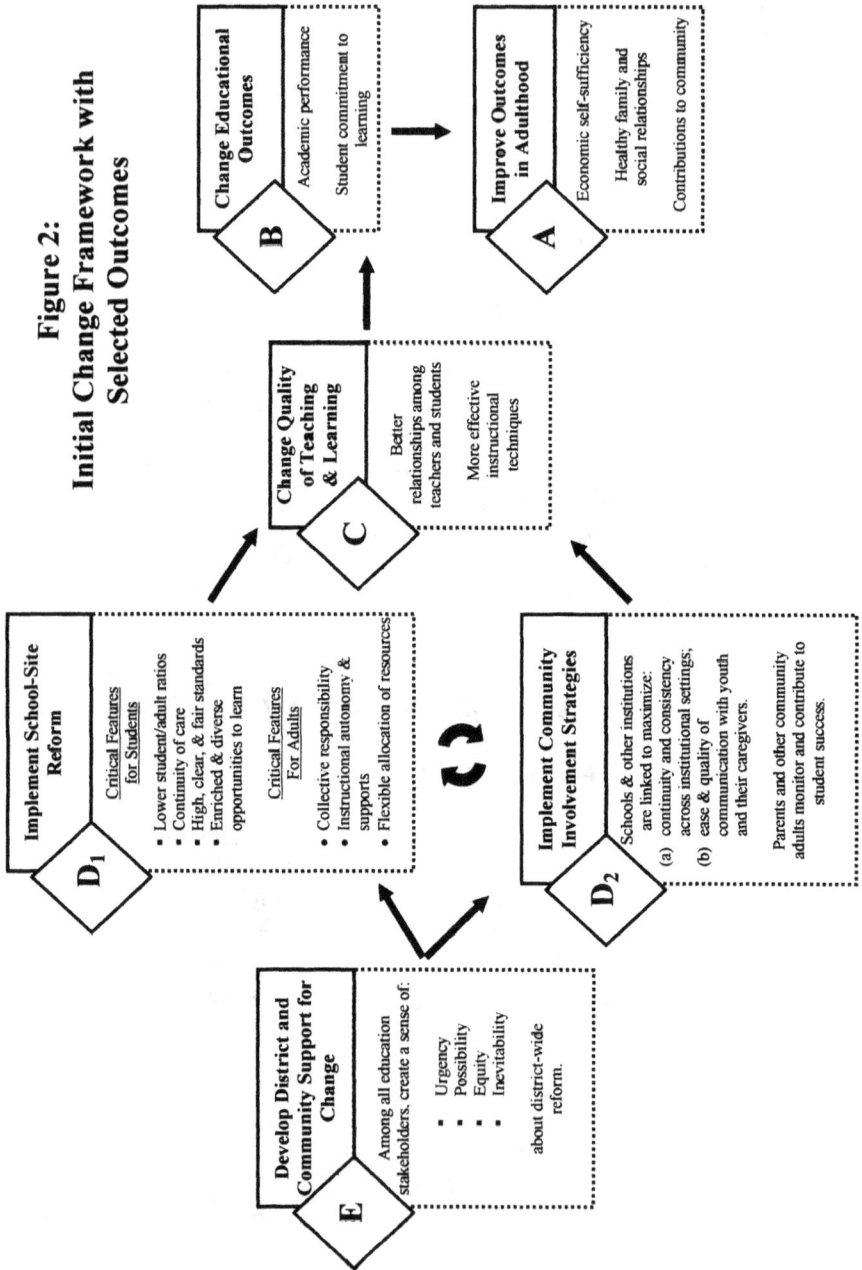

Figure 2:
Initial Change Framework with
Selected Outcomes

Change Educational Outcomes

B

Academic performance

Student commitment to learning

Improve Outcomes in Adulthood

A

Economic self-sufficiency

Healthy family and social relationships

Contributions to community

Change Quality of Teaching & Learning

C

Better relationships among teachers and students

More effective instructional techniques

Implement School-Site Reform

D₁

Critical Features for Students

- Lower student/adult ratios
- Continuity of care
- High, clear, & fair standards
- Enriched & diverse opportunities to learn

Critical Features For Adults

• Collective responsibility
• Instructional autonomy & supports
• Flexible allocation of resources

Implement Community Involvement Strategies

D₂

Schools & other institutions are linked to maximize:

(a) continuity and consistency across institutional settings;

(b) ease & quality of communication with youth and their caregivers.

Parents and other community adults monitor and contribute to student success.

Develop District and Community Support for Change

E

Among all education stakeholders, create a sense of:

- Urgency
- Possibility
- Equity
- Inevitability

about district-wide reform.

ticular change framework reflects IRRE's and others' synthesis of research on youth and organizational development, intensive observation of successful urban schools, and developing expertise in change at the school and district levels. Key elements of this framework are discussed in more detail in IRRE (1996). The framework is presented here to illustrate the characteristics and utility of an imported change framework, not to argue for its validity in relation to other possible change frameworks.

In some circumstances, the scope and/or goals of an initiative demand that local stakeholders generate their own initial change framework; for example, when there is not a credible knowledge base or broad external consensus about what the important outcomes are, or about what best practices contribute to these outcomes. In the field of education reform, however, our own and others' experience suggest there are clear advantages to importing a change framework (Bodilly, 1996; Fashola & Slavin, 1997; Stringfield, et al., 1997). First, less is more in both planning and implementing change. Comprehensive reform becomes more tractable when a change framework with a few key elements can serve as a lens for examining current practices and planning future ones. Second, importing a change framework directs early discussions toward common goals and understandings of what needs to be done and away from self-protective explanations for what is currently done. Third, the imported change framework helps attach the reform agenda to a credible and testable knowledge base and detach it from particular personalities and positions.

In our experience, the risks of using an "imported" change framework to launch the local planning process accrue when the process for engaging stakeholders in a dialogue around the change framework is not carefully thought through.To ensure that a change framework brought in from the outside achieves the credibility among local stakeholders it needs to function effectively, the process must give all stakeholders the time and support to clearly understand each element in the framework.

Case example. An educational roundtable was convened by a local investment partner for "anchor" stakeholders (school board, superintendent and senior management, teacher association, and community leaders, including local foundation investors). This roundtable was an intensive, 2-day retreat during which the imported change framework was studied; dialogue and discussion with the change framework's authors occurred; and stakeholders interacted with teachers, students, administrators, and parents from urban schools where the key elements of the change framework were already in place. Once the anchor stakeholders agreed that the change framework was consistent with and advanced their district's and community's goals, these same roundtables were replicated for teacher, staff, and parent representatives from approximately 10 schools in the first cluster scheduled to implement the reform initiative. Finally, these representatives and anchor stakeholders helped plan and implement a final set of roundtables for the full school staff and interested parents at each school site.

We next describe the initial change framework in greater detail and then clarify the steps in the planning process that convert this framework into a local theory of change that can guide the implementation and the evaluation of a specific initiative.

An Initial Change Framework for Urban School District Reform[3]

Figure 2 includes key elements (Elements A–E) of the framework and key outcomes associated with each. We now walk through these elements, starting with the long-term outcomes and working backward toward the earliest outcomes included in the change framework shown in Figure 2.

Improve outcomes in adulthood (Element A).   What are the ultimate goals of this reform effort? These three outcomes—economic self-sufficiency, healthy family and social relationships, and contributions to community—represent three accomplishments that most of us would agree mark successful transition to adulthood and that research has shown are linked to earlier accomplishments during the school-aged years (for a review of this literature, see Connell, Aber, & Walker, 1995).

Change educational outcomes (Element B).   To help our students achieve these outcomes as adults, what educational outcomes should we focus on while they are in school? Longitudinal research (on urban students) has shown two sets of outcomes to be most strongly predictive of the adult outcomes in the framework: (a) how students do in school academically and (b) how committed they are to their education (Bishop, 1995; Comer, 1988; Connell, 1994; Connell, Spencer, & Aber, 1994; Dryfoos, 1990;

---

[3]Research evidence for the inclusion of the outcomes and linkages in this framework is summarized in IRRE (1996). Primary source citations are also available in this online publication www.kckps.k12.ks.us/documents/ftf_wp/cover.html.

Rumberger, 1987, 1995). By including these research-based and common-sense outcomes in the change framework, reform efforts focus on outcomes that have clear, long-term payoffs and are within the reach of the educational system that is undergoing change.

Change quality of teaching and learning (Element C).   What will it take to improve these educational outcomes? Again, we turn to research and common sense: Change in teaching and learning is the key proximal predictor of change in student performance and commitment. Specifically, change must occur in the everyday lives of students in their classrooms and schools. Change must occur in how and what students are learning (Darling-Hammond, 1997; Felner et al., 1997; Newmann, Marks, & Gamoran, 1995; Newmann & Wehlage, 1995) and in the quality of their relationships to each other and to the adults with whom they interact (e.g., Swanson, Mehan, & Hubbard, 1995; Voelkl, 1995; Wynne & Walberg, 1995).

Implement school site-reform and community involvement strategies (Element D).   For teaching and learning to change in all classrooms for all students, schools will have to be organized differently, school policies and practices will need to change, and new supports will need to be provided for both students and adults (Darling-Hammond, 1997; Howley, 1989; Howley & Huang, 1991; Lee & Smith, 1994a, 1994b; Lee, Smith, & Croninger, 1995). In addition, strategies that increase—and make more meaningful—the involvement of adults, especially parents, from the community and that increase the involvement of other institutions in the community in supporting student success will increase the effectiveness of changes inside the school walls (Haynes, Comer, & Hamilton-Lee, 1989a, 1989b).

Develop district and community supports for change (Element E).   If all these changes have any chance of being implemented and sustained, leaders in the school district and in the community will need to spark, fuel, and monitor the change process at both the school and the community levels. Through its actions, the district leadership (superintendents, teachers association leaders, and boards of education) and other key community leaders must create the conditions that convince stakeholders in the schools themselves, and in the community, that they are expected, empowered, and equipped to implement the change strategies just described.

The key elements and outcomes in Figure 2 remain at a level of abstraction intended to create and sustain consensus around this initial change framework among diverse stakeholders in the reform initiative. The links between them are grounded in the school reform, educational, and child development literatures. They provide credible fundamentals to which everyone can subscribe, while retaining flexibility around implementation strategies. At the same time, the specificity of the framework's outcomes as they are presented in Figure 2 encourages stakeholders to come to grips with what the change process will need to accomplish, its scope and its priorities.

> *Case example.* The district leadership (superintendent, school board, and teachers' association) has committed itself to support the implementation of the critical features of school restructuring shown in Element D of the change framework (see Figure 2). The implementation schedule includes a full year of planning and capacity building for each of the 48 schools before initial implementation of these seven critical features. The first 10 schools have begun implementation. During their planning and capacity building year, all 10 elementary, middle, and high schools examined their current structure and practices through the lens of the seven critical features and developed their plans for improvement. However, their tactics for realigning their current structures and practice and developing the capacity for new practices to get these conditions in place differ markedly, across level (i.e., elementary, middle, and high school) and within level (e.g., between the two middle schools).

Step 2: Selecting Indicators, Populations, Thresholds, and Timelines: The IPTT Process

Once the initial change framework is clear and compelling to key stakeholders, the fleshing out of the "local" theory of change can begin. For this to occur, stakeholders will need to reach consensus around four key questions pertaining to *each* element of the change framework (Figure 2), beginning with Element A and finishing with Element E:

1. What indicators will tell us that this element's outcomes are changing?
2. Which target populations (of people, organizations, or settings) should be showing change on these indicators?
3. How much change in these indicators is good enough?
4. How long do we think it will take to achieve these thresholds?

Figures 3–8 present sample answers to these questions, drawn from our own and others' written work as well as our ongoing consulting work in support of district-wide and school-site reform in urban school districts (e.g., Christman, Foley, Passantino, & Mordecai-Phillips, 1998; Connell, Aber & Walker, 1995; Goertz, Floden, & O'Day, 1995; McLaughlin, 1993; Miles & Darling-Hammond, 1997; Newmann & Wehlage, 1995; Odden & Wohlstetter, 1995; Simmons & Resnick, 1993). Each of the next six figures (Figures 3–8) presents one element (A–E, respectively) of the change framework shown in Figure 2. For each key outcome in that element, the figure lists specific indicators of that outcome and the target population(s) in which that indicator would be assessed. Also included (in Figures 3–8) are examples of *thresholds*—how good is good enough on that indicator—and a timeline, which represents the stakeholders' goal for when the thresholds will be achieved. We next describe each of these steps in the planning process and discuss some issues involved in making these decisions.

Indicators. This step requires stakeholders to build consensus around what they mean by each outcome for each element in the change framework. For example, stakeholders may easily agree to aim for an outcome of improved "academic performance" (Element B), but retain completely different mental pictures of what that will mean for their students—Grades? Enrollment in advanced courses? Retention rates? Indicators need to be specific enough so that *all* stakeholders can answer questions such as

- What are we looking at to decide whether students are performing well?
- How will we know whether the quality of student learning is different?
- How can I find out whether ongoing instructional improvement is going on in a school?
- What will show me whether the superintendent, school board, and union leadership are really behind this initiative?

Target populations (people, organizations, and settings). Once stakeholders agree how the indicators will define the key outcomes under each element in the change framework, the question becomes where they should see them. In what groups of people? For what organizations? In what settings? As can be seen in Figures 3–8, target populations vary depending on the outcome involved: Changes in educational outcomes (Element B) and outcomes in adult-

Figure 3: Improve Outcomes in Adulthood

A

OUTCOME: Economic Self-Sufficiency

INDICATOR 1: Household income
TARGET POPULATION: All students in the district
THRESHOLD: As adults, students who participated in the initiative are better able to support themselves and their families.

INDICATOR 2: Employment or education status
TARGET POPULATION: All students in the district
THRESHOLD: As adults, students who participated in the initiative are more likely to be in or training for decent jobs.

TIMEFRAME 1 & 2: Post-graduation for students with four years of exposure to the initiative

OUTCOME: Healthy Family and Social Relationships

INDICATOR 1: Physical and mental health
TARGET POPULATION: All students in the district
THRESHOLD: Students who participated in the initiative are more likely to grow up to be physically and mentally healthy as adults.

INDICATOR 2: Child rearing and support network
TARGET POPULATION: All students in the district
THRESHOLD: Students who participated in the initiative grow up to be better caregivers for their children and have more positive and dependable family and friendship networks.

TIMEFRAME 1 & 2: Post-graduation for students with four years of exposure to the initiative

OUTCOME: Contributions to Community

INDICATOR 1: Citizenship and community involvement
TARGET POPULATION: All students in the district
THRESHOLD: As adults, students who participated in the initiative are more likely to contribute to their community.

TIMEFRAME 1: Post-graduation for students with four years of exposure to the initiative

Figure 4: Change Educational Outcomes

B

OUTCOME: Academic Performance

INDICATOR 1: Reading and Math Achievement Test Scores
TARGET POPULATION: All students in the district
THRESHOLDS:
1. 60% of students in the district for more than one year score above the national average on math and reading.
2. Less than 5% score in the bottom quartile on either math or reading for more than one year following enrollment in the district.

TIMEFRAME 1: Within five years from implementation of the school-site reform (D_1) and the community involvement strategies (D_2).

OUTCOME: Student Commitment to Learning

INDICATOR 1: Attendance
TARGET POPULATION: All students in the district
THRESHOLDS:
1. 80% of students in the district for more than one year miss no more than one day per month of school.
2. No more than 5% of students in the district for more than one year miss more than one day per week of school.

INDICATOR 2: Graduation Rate
TARGET POPULATION: All students in the district
THRESHOLDS: 90% of district students graduate within five years of entering high school.

TIMEFRAME 1 & 2: Within five years from implementation of the school-site reform (D_1) and the community involvement strategies (D_2).

Figure 5: Change Quality of Teaching and Learning

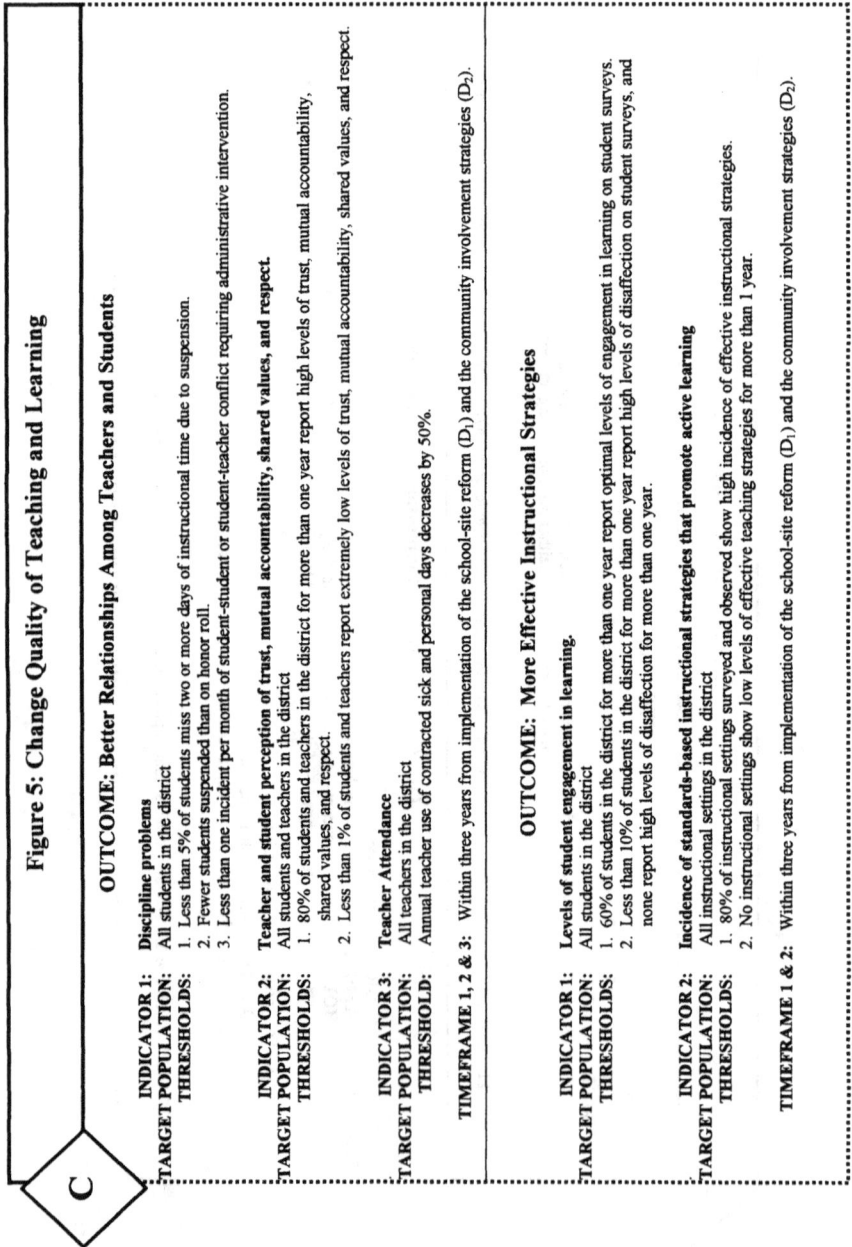

C

OUTCOME: Better Relationships Among Teachers and Students

INDICATOR 1: **Discipline problems**
TARGET POPULATION: All students in the district
THRESHOLDS:
1. Less than 5% of students miss two or more days of instructional time due to suspension.
2. Fewer students suspended than on honor roll.
3. Less than one incident per month of student-student or student-teacher conflict requiring administrative intervention.

INDICATOR 2: **Teacher and student perception of trust, mutual accountability, shared values, and respect.**
TARGET POPULATION: All students and teachers in the district
THRESHOLDS:
1. 80% of students and teachers in the district for more than one year report high levels of trust, mutual accountability, shared values, and respect.
2. Less than 1% of students and teachers report extremely low levels of trust, mutual accountability, shared values, and respect.

INDICATOR 3: **Teacher Attendance**
TARGET POPULATION: All teachers in the district
THRESHOLD: Annual teacher use of contracted sick and personal days decreases by 50%.

TIMEFRAME 1, 2 & 3: Within three years from implementation of the school-site reform (D_1) and the community involvement strategies (D_2).

OUTCOME: More Effective Instructional Strategies

INDICATOR 1: **Levels of student engagement in learning.**
TARGET POPULATION: All students in the district
THRESHOLDS:
1. 60% of students in the district for more than one year report optimal levels of engagement in learning on student surveys.
2. Less than 10% of students in the district for more than one year report high levels of disaffection on student surveys, and none report high levels of disaffection for more than one year.

INDICATOR 2: **Incidence of standards-based instructional strategies that promote active learning**
TARGET POPULATION: All instructional settings in the district
THRESHOLDS:
1. 80% of instructional settings surveyed and observed show high incidence of effective instructional strategies.
2. No instructional settings show low levels of effective teaching strategies for more than 1 year.

TIMEFRAME 1 & 2: Within three years from implementation of the school-site reform (D_1) and the community involvement strategies (D_2).

Figure 6: Implement School-Site Reform

CRITICAL FEATURES FOR STUDENTS

OUTCOME: **Lower Student/Adult Ratios During Core Instruction**

INDICATOR 1: Student/adult ratios experienced by students during literacy and mathematics instruction.
TARGET POPULATION: All students in the district during literacy and mathematics instruction.
THRESHOLD: Average ratios experienced during core instruction is less than or equal to 15 to 1 for 90% of students for at least 10 hours per week.

TIMEFRAME 1: Within two years from implementation of the District and Community Supports for Change (E)

OUTCOME: **Provide Continuity of Care Across the School Day and School Years**

INDICATOR 1: Number of "interruptions" to ongoing learning activities over the course of the school day.
TARGET POPULATION: All schools
THRESHOLD: Students experience at least two instructional periods per day of 90 minutes or more.

INDICATOR 2: Number of adults with ongoing relationships with students over multiple years in schools.
TARGET POPULATION: All schools
THRESHOLDS: 1. Same group of at least two adults remain with same students for core instruction over at least two years in elementary school, all three years of middle school, and at least two years of high school.
2. All schools broken into small learning communities of 200 students or less.

TIMEFRAME 1: Within two years from implementation of the District and Community Supports for Change (E)

OUTCOME: **Embrace and Effectively Communicate High, Clear, and Fair Academic and Behavioral Standards**

INDICATOR 1: Student and teacher understanding of academic and behavioral standards and their connections to their work together.
TARGET POPULATION: All students and teachers in the district
THRESHOLDS: 1. 80% of students and teachers in the district for more than one year report and demonstrate clear understanding of high academic and behavioral standards and the connection between the standards and their work.
2. No more than 10% of students or teachers indicate low levels of understanding of standards, and none do so for more than one year.

TIMEFRAME 1: Within two years from implementation of the District and Community Supports for Change (E)

OUTCOME: **Implement Enriched and Diverse Opportunities to Learn, Perform, and Be Recognized**

INDICATOR 1: Instructional strategies used in classrooms reflect demonstrated best practices.
TARGET POPULATION: All schools
THRESHOLD: 70% of students report experiencing enriched and diverse opportunities to learn, perform, and be recognized in their core instructional classes.

TIMEFRAME 1: Within two years from implementation of the District and Community Supports for Change (E)

D₁

105

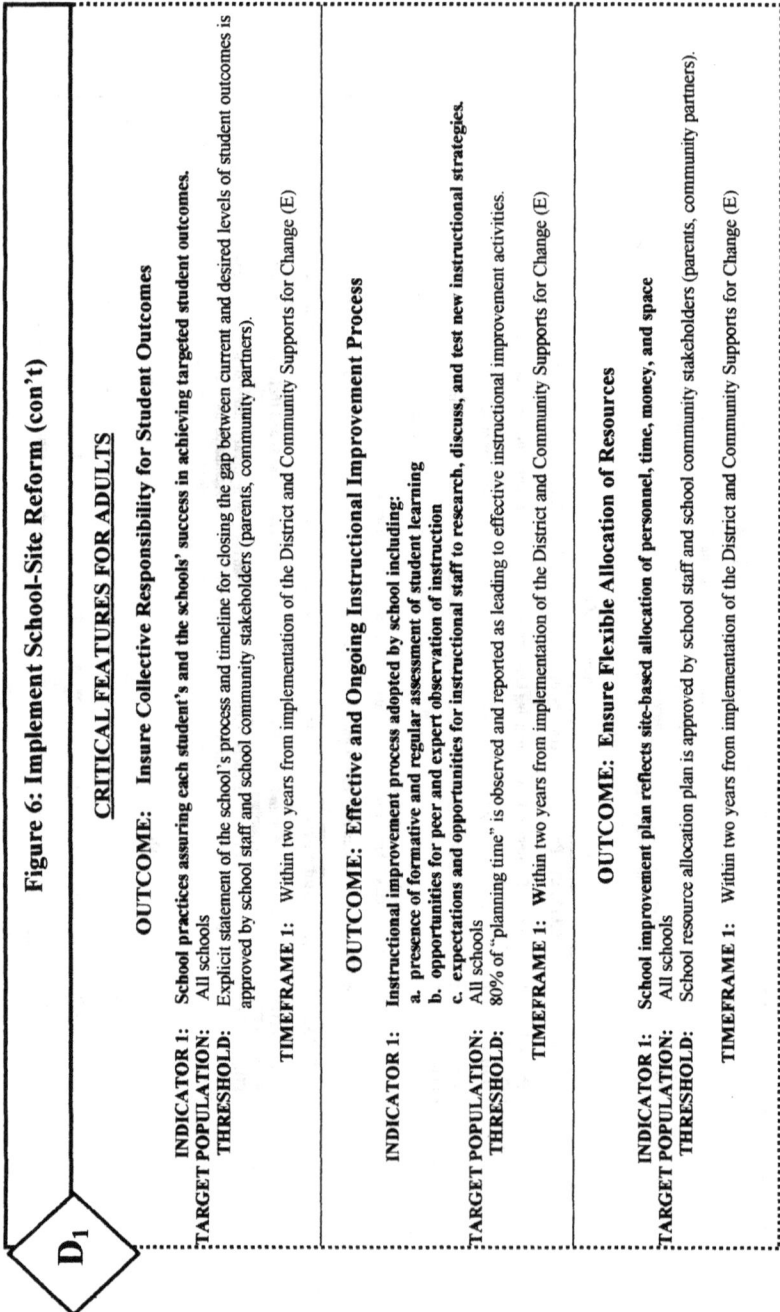

Figure 6: Implement School-Site Reform (con't)

D₁

CRITICAL FEATURES FOR ADULTS

OUTCOME: **Insure Collective Responsibility for Student Outcomes**

INDICATOR 1: School practices assuring each student's and the schools' success in achieving targeted student outcomes.

TARGET POPULATION: All schools

THRESHOLD: Explicit statement of the school's process and timeline for closing the gap between current and desired levels of student outcomes is approved by school staff and school community stakeholders (parents, community partners).

TIMEFRAME 1: Within two years from implementation of the District and Community Supports for Change (E)

OUTCOME: Effective and Ongoing Instructional Improvement Process

INDICATOR 1: Instructional improvement process adopted by school including:
a. presence of formative and regular assessment of student learning
b. opportunities for peer and expert observation of instruction
c. expectations and opportunities for instructional staff to research, discuss, and test new instructional strategies.

TARGET POPULATION: All schools

THRESHOLD: 80% of "planning time" is observed and reported as leading to effective instructional improvement activities.

TIMEFRAME 1: Within two years from implementation of the District and Community Supports for Change (E)

OUTCOME: Ensure Flexible Allocation of Resources

INDICATOR 1: School improvement plan reflects site-based allocation of personnel, time, money, and space

TARGET POPULATION: All schools

THRESHOLD: School resource allocation plan is approved by school staff and school community stakeholders (parents, community partners).

TIMEFRAME 1: Within two years from implementation of the District and Community Supports for Change (E)

Figure 7: Implement Community Involvement Strategies

D₂

OUTCOME: Schools and Other Community Institutions Serving Same Students and Families are Linked in Productive Ways

INDICATOR 1: Mission statements and standards of practice of schools and other institutions.

TARGET POPULATION: District offices; schools; and supporting institutions

THRESHOLDS:
1. Joint mission statements and standards of practice for institutions "sharing" district students reflect commitment to quality, continuity, and consistency.
2. Formal and public commitments by partnering institutions and services to parents and community to do "whatever it takes" to achieve thresholds of success for all students.

INDICATOR 2: Parent and student reports of communication and service quality.

TARGET POPULATION: Parents and students participating in services and supporting programs.

THRESHOLDS:
1. 80% of parents with students involved in partnering institutions or programs report high quality service and communication.
2. No parents or students report low quality service and communication for more than one assessment.

TIMEFRAME 1 & 2: Within two years from implementation of the District and Community Supports for Change (E)

OUTCOME: Parents and Other Community Adults Monitor and Contribute to Student Success.

INDICATOR 1: Parent and community understanding of and commitment to reform.

TARGET POPULATION: Parents and community adults

THRESHOLD: At least 70% of parents and 50% of non-parents know what three key indicators of student success are in their school.

INDICATOR 2: Opportunities for parent and community involvement, at district and school levels, in their students' learning and in specific reform activities.

TARGET POPULATION: District offices; schools; and parents

THRESHOLDS:
1. Written policies in schools encourage and support parent involvement in specific reform activities and in their students' learning.
2. At least 80% of parents can list three positive changes being made in their local school to improve student learning

INDICATOR 3: Parent involvement in student learning.

TARGET POPULATION: Parents

THRESHOLDS:
1. At least 70% of parents report (and students confirm) they have seen, talked about, and/or helped with their son's or daughter's work at least three times in the last week.
2. 95% of parents surveyed know the name of one or more teachers, and have been contacted personally by their child's teacher(s) one or more times each of the past two semesters.

TIMEFRAME 1, 2 & 3: One-two years from implementation of the District and Community Supports for Change (E)

107

Figure 8: District and Community Supports for Change

E

OUTCOME: Create A Sense of Urgency among Education Stakeholders: The Risk of Business as Usual Is Greater Than the Risk of Making These Changes for <u>All</u> Stakeholders.

INDICATOR 1: Public presentations by the superintendent and key educational and community leaders

TARGET POPULATION: Board of education, district offices and personnel, key community stakeholder groups, and teacher association leadership.

THRESHOLDS:
1. Board, teacher association leadership, and superintendent issue a "call to arms" report and endorse adoption of the change framework.
2. "Call to arms" report includes: current levels on key indicators of student outcomes with implications for students and the community, and threats posed by business as usual to students, community, and society.
3. Positive media coverage of superintendent's and key leaders' "Call to arms" report.
4. Major community stakeholder groups accept "Call to arms" report and endorse the change framework.

TIMEFRAME 1: Throughout the year before initial implementation of the school site reform (D_1) and community involvement strategies (D_2).

OUTCOME: Create a Sense of Possibility among Education Stakeholders: They Believe Change in the validity of the change framework at the school and school community level

A. External evidence supports the validity of the change framework at the school and school community level
B. Internal examples of programmatic success suggests the exception can become the rule.
C. Flexible allocation of resources is possible so schools can do what it takes to implement the change framework.

INDICATOR 1: Key stakeholder groups' involvement in and reaction to structured discussion of change framework as guide for the overall district improvement plan.

TARGET POPULATION: Board of education, district offices and personnel, key community stakeholder groups, and teacher association leadership.

THRESHOLDS:
1. Events planned for all schools and key stakeholder groups that incorporate opportunities for exposure to and discussion of the validity of the change framework.
2. At least 80% of each stakeholder group surveyed after participation in discussions is aware of key elements in the framework.
3. At least 50% of participants in each stakeholder group expresses positive attitudes toward implementing and achieving the key elements in the framework.
4. All stakeholder participants can provide local and national examples of successful school-site reform and community involvement strategies currently in place.
5. All stakeholder participants can articulate important next steps for them to take to move the change process forward

INDICATOR 2: Statement of school sites' opportunities and parameters for allocating personnel, time, money, and space to implement change framework.

TARGET POPULATION: Board of education, district offices and personnel, key community stakeholder groups, and teacher association leadership.

THRESHOLD: 70% of school staff and other school community stakeholders believe they have adequate and flexible enough allocation of resources to make effective implementation of school-site reform and community involvement strategies feasible.

TIMEFRAME 1 & 2: The year before initial implementation of the school site reform (D_1) and community involvement strategies (D_2).

Figure 8: District and Community Supports for Change (con't)

E

OUTCOME: Create a Sense of Equity among Education Stakeholders

A. Shift significant central office resources to direct support of school level reform.

B. Assure that planning and capacity building resources are equally allocated across schools.

C. Guarantee that internal reallocation of resources (including keeping, eliminating, and changing existing programs) is determined based on what it takes to close the gap between current and desired student outcomes at the school sites and across the district.

INDICATOR: Job descriptions of district staff and allocation of central office staff and funds to direct support of school planning and capacity building.

TARGET POPULATION: District offices and personnel

THRESHOLDS:
1. 80% of associate superintendent's time is dedicated to implementing district supports for reform.
2. 80% of all curriculum specialists' time is dedicated to support individual schools to do whatever it takes to have the change framework implemented successfully at each site.

INDICATOR: Board of education, superintendent, external funders, and teacher association resolutions, policy statements, and contracts.

TARGET POPULATION: Board of education, district offices and personnel, and teacher association leadership

THRESHOLDS:
1. Events planned for all schools and key stakeholder groups that incorporate opportunities for exposure to and discussion of evidence for success and exemplars of key elements of change framework (D.C.B.A).
2. Resource allocation guaranteed to assure that school improvement plans can all meet the same implementation standards.

TIMEFRAME: The year before initial implementation of the school site reform (D_1) and community involvement strategies (D_2).

OUTCOME: Create A Sense of Inevitability Among Education Stakeholders

A. Establish public district-wide five-year commitments on student outcomes that district leadership is accountable for producing

B. Obtain public commitments of board, district leadership, community leadership, and teacher association leadership to support implementation of change framework

C. Obtain necessary outside resources and external monitoring process to support initial planning and capacity building efforts

D. Develop phase-in strategy and timeline for all schools in the district

INDICATOR: Board of education, superintendent, and teacher association policy statements

TARGET POPULATION: Board of education, district offices and personnel, key community stakeholder groups, and teacher association leadership

THRESHOLDS:
1. Board approval and public dissemination of five-year commitments
2. Joint and individual public statements in writing by stakeholder groups supporting implementation of change framework
3. Plan that includes which schools will be implementing when and with what resources

INDICATOR: District budget and outside grants

TARGET POPULATION: District offices, schools and supporting institutions, and parents

THRESHOLDS:
1. Adequate resources committed to complete planning and capacity building year for district.
2. Mutual accountability plan with stated accomplishments and responsibilities triggers continued external funding.

TIMEFRAME: The year before initial implementation of the school site reform (D_1) and community involvement strategies (D_2).

109

hood (Element A) should be observed in the total student population of the district if the initiative is district wide.[4] Structural changes implemented to achieve school-site reform (Element D_1) should occur *in all schools*. Changes in policies to develop district and community supports for change (Element E) should occur at the board of education, in all community stakeholder groups, and in the superintendent's office.

Thresholds.   Once stakeholders have specified the indicators for all outcomes in a particular key element (A, B, C, D, or E) and chosen their target populations, they can address the question, how good is good enough on each indicator? Stakeholders will need to start with educational outcomes (Element B)[5], then move to quality of teaching and learning (Element C), and so on. It is only when they know how much change they want in student performance and commitment that they can know how much change they need in what, and how, students are taught and what kinds of relationships students and teachers must develop. Therefore, setting change thresholds requires baseline assessments early on in the planning process of indicators for key outcomes in the change framework.

In our experience, discussions among stakeholders about change thresholds elevate the planning process to a change-*making* activity. Achieving consensus on the question of how good is good enough means changing most stakeholders' mindsets about what needs to be done and what it is really going to take to do it. Without district and community leaders working to change their own and others' mindsets, the planning process loses traction. Without this traction, the energy needed to move through the next steps of the planning process will dissipate.

Timelines.   The next step is to set preliminary timelines for achieving the newly defined thresholds for each of the key elements. How long it will take an urban school district to achieve its thresholds is dependent on an array of forces, some more controllable than others (e.g., allocation of discre-

---

[4]Obviously, if the initiative is restricted to a set of schools or a single school, this target population would narrow; if the theory of change was being articulated for a specific program that served a limited number of students within a school or across the district, the target population would be adjusted accordingly.

[5]Discussion of how good is good enough on the adult outcomes (Element A) can generate thresholds such as those shown in Figures 4–8, but more specific thresholds than those presented in Figure 3 would require the knowledge of community conditions and other supports available for students outside the purview of even the broadest educational reform initiative.

tionary resources vs. cuts in state-level funding). But, visible deadlines for achieving the thresholds on educational outcomes (Element B) appear to be a necessary (but not a sufficient) condition to get specific action strategies that are linked to the early outcomes articulated and to get resources reallocated to those strategies.

On the other hand, the timelines for later outcomes must be contingent on achieving earlier ones. For example, we should see threshold levels in the quality of teaching and learning (Element C) achieved within X years after implementation of the critical features of school-site reform (Element D). The sample timelines in Figures 3–8 reflect our own ongoing work with small to medium-sized urban school districts, which are either beginning to put district and community supports for change (Element E) in place or are in the earliest steps of implementing school-site reform (Element D_1) and community involvement strategies (Element D_2).

> *Case example.* Five-year change thresholds have been set for the entire school district in the areas of reading, math, student attendance, and disciplinary actions (Figure 2, Element B, and Figure 4). These outcomes, target populations, indicators, and thresholds were developed jointly by a District Improvement Planning Committee—a group of 40–50 community stakeholders representing parents, community leaders, and district employees—and were refined by an internal committee of central office staff and school-level administrators. The recommendations of these committees were vetted internally in the district and externally with and by the board of education, senior district management, and teacher association leadership. School-level administrators and stakeholders have converted these 5-year change thresholds to annual targets for each school.
>
> In the past year, data on the quality of teaching and learning (Figure 2, Element B), including student perceptions and classroom observations of instructional practices and student engagement, were being examined by school staff as part of their collective professional development activities. Specific indicators of the quality of instruction and teacher relationships were being targeted and then used to guide school improvement plans. These plans focused on the implementation of school restructuring and change in community involvement, the two key elements in Element D of the change framework.

Step 3: Developing Action Strategies to Strengthen District and Community Supports for Change (Element E)

With the indicators, populations, thresholds, and timelines (IPTT) completed, stakeholders must next identify local action strategies for putting the district and community supports for change (Element E) in place. For example, to provide district and community leaders the opportunity "to create a community-wide sense of urgency":

1. Data will be collected and analyzed to tell these leaders where students stand now on educational outcomes (Element B).
2. Tools will be developed for creating dialogue, in different settings, about what these results mean for their students, for the district, and for the community.

Other activities will have to be planned as well to broaden awareness and knowledge of the change framework and the evidence supporting the links among its elements.

These action strategies and others become part of the theory of change along with the change framework's key elements and outcomes and the IPTT information generated thus far through the planning process. These action strategies must be prioritized and sequenced, and timelines based on existing local conditions and resource considerations must be established for their implementation (see next section). Similar to the IPTT steps, the links between these action strategies and the achievement of the district and community supports for change (Element E) must be found plausible by the stakeholders responsible for implementing them. Questions to consider include

- If we do these things, will we create district and community supports for change (Element E), sufficient to launch school site-reform and community involvement strategies (Elements D_1 and D_2, respectively) such as those in Figures 6 and 7?
- Have we specified these action strategies sufficiently so that we can tell if they are being implemented properly?

Case example. The education roundtables described earlier are used to create a sense of "urgency and possibility" (Element E) among education stakeholders. The major focus of the roundtable experience was the presentation of data about students in school districts similar to the participating districts (in the initial leadership roundtable) and then data on this district's own students. Drawing on national, longitudinal research on urban students, IRRE staff led discussions on the implications of these current levels of student performance for these students' and their communities' future well-being and risk.

After this, educational stakeholders heard from, and interacted directly with, students, teachers, and administrators from urban schools serving similar student populations, some of whom had worked with IRRE, whereas others who had not. All of these schools, however, were implementing the critical features of the change framework (Element D) and had achieved, or were on their way to achieving, performance levels comparable to suburban school districts.

Step 4: Final Implementation Planning

Resource mapping.   The penultimate step before implementation is to determine whether sufficient resources are available, or are obtainable, to implement the action strategies identified in the previous step. Resource issues will have already shaped the selection of these action strategies, their prioritization, and the timelines. However, it is at this step of the planning process that a final check of whether those responsible for implementing the initial action strategies truly believe they have, or can obtain, adequate resources, including money, time, human capacity, and political will, to do what they have promised. If not, they must find access to these additional resources or alter thresholds and timelines.

This decision to either lower expectations or raise additional resources before moving ahead is a hard but critical choice for reform initiatives. Many reform initiatives do not even recognize the gap between resources and expectations. Some recognize the gap and charge ahead anyway. In both cases, a venture that is fraught with risks, even when resources appear adequate, becomes a suicide mission when people know the resources are not. For example, if a superintendent cannot really allocate the time to work with the board of education and leaders of the teachers association to learn about the change framework, the chance of achieving adequate district and community supports for change (Element E) dwindles.

Achieving threshold levels of district and community supports for change (Element E) is also doubtful if

- Clear and compelling information about where students stand on educational outcomes (Element B) is not available for use by district and community leaders.
- Tools for having dialogue and getting information out about why the desired thresholds for these outcomes are urgently needed and how they can be achieved are not available to stakeholders.

Resource mapping requires that all stakeholders and that each stakeholder responsible for implementation of the action strategies address the following questions:

1. What do we need to get these action strategies implemented?
2. What do we now have?
3. How can we close the gap?

Mutual accountability plan (MAP). The MAP describes a governance structure, monitoring process, and work plan for the implementation of the initiative. Who will be involved in the ongoing monitoring of the plan and making adjustments based on interim results? What process will be used to hold individuals, groups, and organizations accountable? The work plan should include the specific activities that comprise the action strategies, the persons responsible to the governing body for getting them done, the funding sources for these activities, and the timelines and benchmarks for tracking their completion.

> *Case example.* An executive committee for the education reform initiative developed a "mutual accountability plan," and assigned responsibility for the completion of these activities to the three partners: a local foundation funder, a school district representative, and a technical assistance provider (IRRE). The mutual accountability plan includes benchmarks describing what constitutes satisfactory completion of key activities under each action strategy, timelines for doing so, and source(s) of funds, people, and facilities. The committee conducts formal reviews of progress every 6 months and confers once a month to track short-term progress. Funding from foundation and district sources is contingent on these formal reviews, which also lead to the reallocation of funds when adjustments are needed.
>
> The mutual accountability plan is updated as the initiative proceeds from left to right through the elements of the change framework. For example, upcoming additions to the mutual accountability plan will include
>
> - Annual implementation thresholds—statements of how much change from baseline assessments of implementation of the key elements in Element D is expected.
> - What resource and policy realignments and other reform activities will be reviewed once actual change data are compared to expected change thresholds.

SUMMARY AND CONCLUDING COMMENTS

In another article (Connell & Klem, 1996) we discussed how this theory of change approach affects and, we believe, improves the evaluation of education reform initiatives. In our final comments here, we focus on why we think this planning process can improve the quality and "implementability" of urban education reform strategies; again, we use our case example to illustrate these points.

First, our own and others' experience working in urban schools and districts tells us that plans for reform are improved when district, community and building leaders, and then broader groups of stakeholders begin with an initial change framework grounded in credible and understandable evidence. Such a framework could help launch a reform effort from many platforms. These include community-based advocacy groups; a single school's staff or administration; charter school legislation; state or federal initiatives; or, as in our case example, a partnership among school district leadership, a local investment partner, and a national consulting firm.

Regardless of the impetus for the reform initiative or its scale (single school or entire district), Elements A through D in a framework such as that shown in Figure 2 can become the touchstones that focus local planning. They become the things that stakeholders come to believe must happen if meaningful change in the life chances of its' students is going to occur. Without these touchstones, or ones like them, we and others have observed planning processes guided less by what needs to be done than by protecting the sacred cows of business as usual. We have found that a change framework such as that shown in Figure 2 has already helped our case example withstand the urges to return to business as usual over the course of three changes in its' superintendent during the planning and capacity building process. The district's theory of change has also been used to fend off well-intentioned, but distracting, program and funding opportunities in favor of staying the course its theory of change provides.

Implementation is a more complicated issue. As stakeholders in our case example struggle to find collective answers to the questions posed by the theory of change planning process, new working relationships have been formed and new leaders have emerged within and across key stakeholder groups—among teachers, parents, students, administrators, the board, and other community members. These new relationships are being forged through collective learning about, and building a commitment to, a clear, ambitious, and realistic vision of what constitutes

- Good performance for their students.
- High quality classroom practice.
- Effective school organization and community involvement.
- Sufficient district and community supports for change.

These new working relationships are being sorely tested by the hard work of implementing these commitments: hard work that has defeated many a plausible plan for single school reform, much less district reform. Through the focused work of making these key decisions and commitments, stakeholders are slowly developing the skill and will that are necessary during implementation to challenge and support each other and their colleagues to

- Choose change-making work over doing what is comfortable and familiar.
- Follow through on commitments made.
- Persist together in overcoming setbacks.

We believe that without these kinds of "behaviors" in the leaders early on and throughout, and in all participants eventually, the implementation of change in our case example, and others that follow, will fall short.

Gaining the investment of many people, an investment that asks them to set aside their own agendas, is always a messy business. It is tempting for school districts to see what will happen if they make smaller-scale change. Unfortunately, we have learned again and again that core and systemic actions are necessary to improve critical outcomes for the majority of students in greatest need. If reform plans continue to disappoint, the deepening cynicism of investors in reform, including the participants themselves, can only make future investments more difficult to obtain. Ultimately, the highest cost of the shortfalls of reform will be to those who should benefit—the students, their families, and their community. With these prospects facing us, consultants and advisors to educational investors must find better and smarter ways of planning and evaluating their investments. We close with several suggestions in this regard.

Our experience with this approach to planning educational reform has surfaced several commonly recognized needs that could be met by educational and psychological consultants. These are listed and described briefly in Table 1. Where this approach challenges our field to think differently, is in how we market and develop our expertise and experience in these areas. Do we explicitly place our services in the context of a change framework, or do we adapt to our client's implicit or explicit theory of change, with little regard for its clarity or quality? Our judgment at this point is that our clients benefit from the structure that initial change frameworks and theory of change planning activities

TABLE 1
Functional Categories of Consultant Supports for District-Level Reform

1. Communication and team building.	• Support, train, and promote healthy team practices. • Change-making strategies. • Communication and listening skills. • Peer coaching. • Group learning strategies.
2. Instructional improvement.	• Develop implementation frameworks to promote standards-based assessment and instruction. • Action research instructional improvement. • Curricular enrichment.
3. School-site change.	• Develop and support school-site planning and implementation strategies for critical features of school-site reform.
4. District leadership support.	• Clarify roles of senior management, teacher association and the board in support of district and school-site reform framework. • Develop and support district restructuring; develop policy and resource realignment strategies.
5. Community and parent support.	• Develop and support strategies for engaging and equipping parents and other community stakeholders to enhance their children's learning and their schools' implementation of its change framework.

provide. Most educational systems we have encountered are sorely tested by this approach. Even for those willing to take the plunge, the benefits of the approach will only be achieved with the support of consultants, support for moving through the process, but more important, support in the design and implementation of the activities necessary to achieve the outcomes in their theory of change. This will require us, as a field, as individuals, and as consulting organizations to specialize, but to do so in cooperative ways both locally and nationally—a mean feat for a highly competitive, fragmented, and decentralized field. Bottom line: as we support and advise our clients to use this type of planning approach to become more efficient, collaborative, and results based in their work, we will have to be ready to do the same.

REFERENCES

Argyris, C. (1993). *Knowledge for action: A guide to overcoming barriers to organizational change.* (Jossey-Bass Management Series & Jossey-Bass Social & Behavioral Series.) San Francisco: Jossey-Bass.

Argyris, C., & Schon, D. A. (1974). *Theory in practice: Increasing professional effectiveness.* (A joint publication in the Jossey-Bass Higher and Adult Education Series and The Jossey-Bass Management Series.) San Francisco: Jossey-Bass.

Bishop, J. J. (1995, June). Improving education: How large are the benefits? Written testimony delivered before a US Senate Subcommittee on September 2, 1995. *Network News and Views, 14*(6), 21–37.

Bodilly, S. J. (1996). *Lessons from the New American Schools Development Corporation's Demonstration Phase.* Santa Monica, CA: RAND.

Christman, J. B., Foley, E., Passantino, C., & Mordecai-Phillips, R. (1998). *Guidance for school improvement in a decentralizing system: How much, what kind and from where?* (Children Achieving: Philadelphia's Education Reform. Progress Report Series 1996–1997.) Philadelphia: Consortium for Policy Research in Education.

Comer, J. P. (1988). Educating poor minority children. *Scientific American, 259,* 48.

Connell, J. P. (1994). *Applying a youth development perspective to the early prediction of African-American males' labor market attachment.* Philadelphia: Public/Private Ventures.

Connell, J. P., Aber, J. L., & Walker, G. (1995). How do urban communities affect youth? Using social science research to inform the design and evaluation of comprehensive community initiatives. In J. P. Connell, A. C. Kubisch, L. B. Schorr, & C. H. Weiss (Eds.), *New approaches to evaluating community initiatives: Concepts, methods, and contexts* (pp. 93–125). Washington, DC: The Aspen Institute.

Connell, J. P., & Klem, A. K. (1996, September). *A theories-of-change approach to evaluating investments in public education.* Paper presented at the meeting of the Independent Sector, Washington, DC.

Connell, J. P., & Kubisch, A. C. (1998). *Applying a theories of change approach to the design and evaluation of comprehensive community initiatives: Progress, prospects, and problems.* Washington, DC: The Aspen Institute.

Connell, J. P., Spencer, M. B., & Aber, J. L. (1994). Educational risk and resilience in African-American youth: Context, self, action, and outcomes in school. *Child Development, 65,* 493–506.

Darling-Hammond, L. (1997). *The right to learn: A blueprint for creating schools that work.* San Francisco: Jossey-Bass.

Dryfoos, J. G. (1990). *Adolescents at risk: Prevalence and prevention.* New York: Oxford University Press.

Fashola, O. S., & Slavin, R. E. (1997). *Effective and replicable programs for students placed at risk in elementary and middle schools.* Baltimore, MD: Johns Hopkins University.

Felner, R. D., Jackson, A. W., Kasak, D., Mulhall, P., Brand, S., & Flowers, N. (1997, March). The impact of school reform for the middle years: Longitudinal study of a network engaged in Turning Points-Based Comprehensive School Transformation. *Phi Delta Kappan, 78*(7), 530–550.

Fetterman, D. M., Kaftarian, S. J., & Wandersman, A. (1995). *Empowerment evaluation: Knowledge and tools for self-assessment and accountability.* Newbury Park, CA: Sage.

Goertz, M. E., Floden, R. E., & O'Day, J. (1995). *Studies of education reform: Systemic reform. Volume 1: Findings and conclusions* (CPRE Research Report Series Report #35A). Philadelphia: Consortium for Policy Research in Education.

Haynes, N. M., Comer, J. P., & Hamilton-Lee, M. (1989a). School climate enhancement through parental involvement. *Journal of School Psychology, 27,* 87–90.

Haynes, N. M., Comer, J. P., & Hamilton-Lee, M. (1989b). The effects of parental involvement on student performance. *Educational and Psychological Research, 8,* 291–299.

Howley, C. B. (1989). Synthesis of the effects of school and district size: What research says about achievement in small schools and school districts. *Journal of Rural and Small Schools, 4,* 2–12.

Howley, C. B., & Huang, G. (1991, July). Extracurricular participation and achievement: School size as possible mediator of SES influence among individual students. *Resources in Education,* 1–36.

Hustedde, R., & Score, M. (1995). Force-field analysis: Incorporating critical thinking in goal setting. *CD Practice, 4,* 1–7.

Institute for Research and Reform in Education. (1996). *First Things First: Defining, implementing, and evaluating the critical features of successful school site reform.* (White paper prepared for the E. M. Kauffman Foundation.) Kansas City, MO: E. M. Kauffman Foundation.

Julian, D. A., Jones, A., & Deyo, D. (1995). Open systems evaluation and the logic model: Program planning and evaluation tools. *Evaluation and Program Planning, 18,* 333–341.

Kaufman, R. & Herman, J. (1991). *Strategic planning in education: Rethinking, restructuring, and revitalizing.* Lancaster, PA: Technomic.

Lee, V. E., & Smith, J. B. (1994a). *Effects of high school restructuring and size on gains in achievement and engagement for early secondary school students.* Madison, WI: Center on Organization and Restructuring of Schools.

Lee, V. E., & Smith, J. B. (1994b). High school restructuring and student achievement: A new study finds strong links. *Issues in Restructuring Schools, 7,* 1–5. Madison, WI: Center on the Organization and Restructuring of Schools.

Lee, V. E., Smith, J. B., & Croninger, R. G. (1995). Another look at high school restructuring. *Issues in Restructuring Schools, 9,* 5–10. Madison, WI: Center on the Organization and Restructuring of Schools.

McLaughlin, M. W. (1993). What matters most in teachers' workplace context. In J. W. Little & M. W. McLaughlin (Eds.), *Teachers' work: Individuals, colleagues, and contexts* (pp. 79–103). New York: Teachers College Press.

Miles, K. H., & Darling-Hammond, L. (1997). *Rethinking the allocation of teaching resources: Some lessons from high performing schools* (Consortium for Policy Research in Education Research Report Series RR-38). Philadelphia: Consortium for Policy Research in Education.

Newmann, F. M., Marks, H., & Gamoran, A. (1995, April). *Authentic pedagogy and student performance.* Paper presented at the meeting of the American Education Research Association. San Francisco, CA.

Newmann, F. M., & Wehlage, G. G. (1995). *Successful school restructuring (A report to the public and educators).* Madison, WI: Center on Organization and Restructuring of Schools.

Odden, E. R. & Wohlstetter, P. (1995). Making school-based management work. *Educational Leadership, 52,* 32–36.

Rumberger, R. W. (1987). High school dropouts: A review of issues and evidence. *Review of Educational Research, 57,* 101–121.

Rumberger, R. W. (1995). Dropping out of middle school: A multilevel analysis of students and schools. *American Educational Research Journal, 32,* 583–625.

Simmons, W., & Resnick, L. (1993). Assessment as the catalyst of school reform. *Educational Leadership, 50,* 11–15.

Stringfield, S., Millsap, M. A., Herman, R., Yoder, N., Brigham, N., Nesselrodt, P., Schaffer, E., Karweit, N., Levin, M., & Stevens, R. (1997). *Urban and suburban/rural special strategies for educating disadvantaged children: Final report.* Washington, DC: US Department of Education.

Swanson, M. C., Mehan, H., & Hubbard, L. (1995). The AVID Classroom: Academic and social support for low-achieving students. *Yearbook National Society for the Study of Education* (Vol. 94, pt. 1), 53–69.

Voelkl, K. E. (1995). School warmth, student participation, and achievement. *Journal of Experimental Education, 63,* 127–138.

Weiss, C. H. (1995). Nothing as practical as good theory: Exploring theory-based evaluation for comprehensive community initiatives for children and families. In J. P. Connell, A. C. Kubisch, L. B. Schorr, & C. H. Weiss (Eds.), *New approaches to evaluating community initiatives: Concepts, methods, and contexts* (pp. 65–92). Washington, DC: The Aspen Institute.

Wynne, E. A., & Walberg, H. J. (1995). The virtues of intimacy in education. *Educational Leadership, 53,* 53–54.

James P. Connell is the Cofounder and Director of Research for the Institute for Research and Reform in Education based in Philadelphia. Dr. Connell's research interests and expertise are in schools and communities as contexts for child and youth development and in research methodology. His institute is currently involved in several planning and evaluation efforts involving urban school systems, youth-serving organizations, and communities. He has worked extensively on methods for eliciting, enriching, and validating theories of change guiding child and youth development initiatives in these settings.

Adena M. Klem is a Research Associate at the Institute for Research and Reform in Education. Her research interests and expertise are in the areas of motivation, especially as it pertains to education, and research methodology. As a member of the institute, Dr. Klem is currently involved with various school-site reform efforts as well as documenting the theories of change approach to planning and evaluating urban school systems.

JOURNAL OF EDUCATIONAL AND PSYCHOLOGICAL CONSULTATION, *11*(1), 121–145

Partnerships for Implementing School and Community Prevention Programs

Geoffrey Nelson, Jeannette L. Amio, Isaac Prilleltensky, and Peggy Nickels
Wilfrid Laurier University

The planning and implementation of prevention programs for families and children has shifted towards community-based, multi-component approaches that are rooted in partnerships among diverse stakeholders. We argue that values and partnerships should be central to the planning and implementation of this new approach to prevention programs. Following from these concepts, we propose 6 steps that can guide educational and psychological consultants in the implementation of prevention programs in partnership with other stakeholders. For each step, we identify key tasks, processes, and challenges for consultants. To illustrate these steps, we include examples from our work in prevention initiatives for and with immigrant and refugee children and families.

Recently, there has been a shift away from single-focus, researcher-driven approaches to prevention, to more community-based, multi-component approaches involving many partners (Schorr, 1997). In the new approach, the implementation of the intervention is rooted in community development (Powell & Nelson, 1997), and the evaluation of the intervention uses participatory action research (Nelson, Ochocka, Griffin, & Lord, 1998). Values and partnerships are central to this new approach.

The main objective of this article is to assist educational and psychological consultants in developing value-based partnerships for the effective

Correspondence should be addressed to Geoffrey Nelson, Department of Psychology, Wilfrid Laurier University, Waterloo, ON N2L 3C5. E-mail: gnelson@wlu.ca implementation of prevention programs. To achieve this aim, we prescribe a series of six steps to guide consultation practice: (a) create partnerships, (b) clarify values and vision and derive working principles, (c) identify and merge the strengths of different approaches and partners, (d) define the problem collaboratively, (e) develop the prevention program collaboratively, and (f) research and evaluate the program collaboratively. For each step, we identify key tasks, processes, and challenges. Moreover, we illustrate each of the steps with examples from our experiences as partners in implementing prevention programs for and with immigrant and refugee children.

VALUES AND PARTNERSHIPS

We believe that although values are of central importance to planning and implementing preventive interventions, there has been very little discussion of values in the prevention literature (for an exception, see Prilleltensky, Peirson, & Nelson, 1997). We define *values* as beliefs that guide our actions. Like Shalom Schwartz (1994), we believe that values are principles that illuminate our personal, professional, and civic behavior. We concur with psychologists Mayton, Ball-Rokeach, and Loges (1994), who stated that "values may be defined as enduring prescriptive or proscriptive beliefs that a specific mode of conduct (instrumental value) or end state of existence (terminal value) is preferred to another mode of conduct or end state" (p. 3). We also agree with philosopher John Kekes (1993), who defined values as "humanly caused benefits that human beings provide to others.... By way of illustration, we may say that love and justice are moral goods" (p. 44).

Elsewhere, we have defined five key values for community psychology and prevention: (a) caring and compassion, (b) human diversity, (c) self-determination and participation, (d) health, and (e) social justice (Prilleltensky & Nelson, 1997; Prilleltensky et al., 1997). As community psychologists and as concerned citizens, we endeavor to actualize the five values with the belief that a more just society can result. *Caring and compassion* refers to the genuine and moral concern one has for the well-being of others, whereas *human diversity* speaks to a respect and appreciation for the ability of persons to self-define their identity (Prilleltensky & Nelson, 1997). *Self-determination* and *participation* refer to individuals being able to direct and participate in decisions relevant to their lives, whereas community psychology's definition of *health* entails a preventive and health promoting view of physical and mental wellness (Prilleltensky et al., 1997).

Finally, the equitable allotment of power, resources, and burdens in society defines the term *social justice* (Prilleltensky & Nelson, 1997; Prilleltensky et al., 1997). In Table 1, we summarize the definitions of these values and outline implications for the implementation of prevention programs. In our experiences, an adherence to these community values is not only important for the effective implementation of prevention programs, but also for creating larger social change. Values do not exist in the abstract, but rather are manifested in our day-to-day relationships with other people. It is through our relationships that we "live the values." It is for this reason that we believe that partnership is another essential concept for the implementation of prevention programs. Elsewhere, we have defined partnerships as

> relationships between community psychologists and oppressed groups (and possibly other stakeholders); relationships that strive to advance the values of caring, compassion, community, health, self-determination, participation, power-sharing, human diversity, and social justice for oppressed groups. These values drive both in the processes and the outcomes of partnerships

TABLE 1

Community Psychology Values: Definition and Implications for Partnerships in Program Implementation

Community Values	Definition	Implications for Partnerships in Program Implementation
Caring and compassion.	Showing empathy and concern for the well-being of others.	Form responsive and responsible relationships with stakeholders based on mutual trust, where professionals begin with humility and ensure partners feel safe and valued.
Human diversity.	Appreciating the inherent worth of others and respecting each person's right to define her/his identity.	Build a stakeholder-based approach to implementation that accepts and incorporates their different realities in the process and program.
Self-determination and participation.	Directing and participating in decisions affecting one's own life.	Share power with partners by using open problem solving and shared decision making.
Health.	Preventing and promoting physical and emotional wellness for the individual and the community.	Address the health, personal, and social needs of our partners and build on the strengths of the setting and its members.
Social Justice.	Distributing bargaining power, resources, and burdens in society in an equitable manner.	Work for an equitable distribution of power and resources among partners.

that focus on services and supports, coalitions and social action, and research and evaluation. (Nelson, Prilleltensky, & MacGillivary, in press, p. 3)

Although the concept of partnership draws attention to values, relationships, and processes, partnership can also lead to a bridging of ideas and perspectives.

It is our belief that values and partnerships are central to the implementation of effective prevention programs, but that these concepts have been overlooked in the prevention literature. In the next section, we outline concrete steps for the implementation of prevention programs that place values and partnerships front and center in our conceptualization of the implementation process.

VALUE-BASED PARTNERSHIPS FOR IMPLEMENTING PREVENTION PROGRAMS: SIX STEPS

The six steps that we have identified include key tasks, processes, and challenges for effective prevention program implementation (see Table 2). We illustrate each of these steps with examples from work we have done in community settings with immigrant and refugee families and children. We refer to ourselves in the examples by our first names.

Step 1: Create Partnerships

As defined earlier, the concept of *partnership* that we endorse is grounded in community psychology values and endeavors to put into practice the values in the partnership relationship itself and in the prevention programs for which the partnership is formed. A growing body of research (e.g., MacGillivary & Nelson, 1998; Nelson et al., in press) has reported on relationship qualities that facilitate successful partnerships, including mutual respect, trust, clear communication, self-disclosure, and friendship. Through positive relationships, groups of diverse stakeholders create something larger than a specific prevention program: They build a sense of community, a positive social climate, and an ethos of change in the setting, which promotes the thrust of specific prevention activities (Schorr, 1997). This is not to say that tangible resources are not important for planning preventive interventions. Research indicates that release time for teachers, child care, food and fun activities, an informal working style, and transla-

TABLE 2
Steps in the Implementation of Valued-Based Partnerships for Prevention Program Implementation:
Tasks, Processes, and Challenges

Steps	*Value-Based Tasks and Processes*	*Challenges for Consultants*
Create partnerships.	• Include community residents and service providers from the community where the intervention is to take place. • Create a welcoming and friendly climate for partners.	• Abandon the role of the expert and share power with partners. • Reduce barriers to participation for partners. • Learn to value and build relationships
Clarify values and vision and derive working principles.	• Collaboratively clarify values and vision to guide the project. • Derive working principles (ground rules) for how the group and program should work.	• Engage in self-reflexive analysis of personal values. • Be open to being challenged by partners. • Be aware of value incongruence and strive to reduce it.
Identify and merge the strengths of different partners and approaches.	• Identify and build on strengths of different partners. • Merge deductive/nomothetic and inductive/experiential approaches to planning and implementation.	• Work to overcome self-doubts and mistrust of community members. • Value the experiential knowledge of community partners. • Find common ground and respect differences to bridge the worlds of community members and professionals.
Define the problem collaboratively.	• Collaboratively define and analyze the problem in terms of risk and protective factors at multiple ecological levels. • Focus on the strengths of the community.	• Reconcile differing views and build consensus regarding a prevention program model. • Build ownership and support for program model.
Develop the prevention program collaboratively.	• Collaboratively decide on what type of prevention program to implement. • Ensure that necessary hardware and software are available for program implementation.	• Educate and train partners in research and evaluation. • Be open to learning new perspectives and ways of working from partners. • Clarify roles.
Research and evaluate collaboratively.	• Use both deductive (quantitative) and inductive (qualitative) approaches in program evaluation. • Research and evaluate each of the steps.	• Educate and train partners in research and evaluation. • Learn to see community members as valuable partners in research and evaluation. • Clarify roles of partners.

125

tion services (if needed) are some of the resources required to build partnership relationships (Nelson et al., in press; Peirson & Prilleltensky, 1994).

Who should be a partner?   Partnerships for the implementation of
prevention programs should combine the efforts of two main stakeholder
groups: those traditionally regarded as "experts" sent in to "fix" the focal
problem and those most vulnerable to the problem itself. These two groups
have been referred to as *outsiders* and *insiders,* respectively (Dimock, 1992),
or the *formal* and *informal* sectors, respectively (Narayan, 1999). In a school
setting, the formal sector includes consultants, teachers, psychologists, human service providers, and administrators, whereas students and parents
comprise the informal sector. Rarely are parents or students recruited to
participate in planning prevention programs. We argue that both sectors
need to be involved in prevention program planning and implementation.

Why should we form partnerships?   As community psychologists,
we believe that value-based partnerships should exist for the ultimate
benefit of those living in disadvantaged conditions. In other words, we
believe that working with people who are disadvantaged in partnerships
for prevention is a moral imperative based on the values that we outlined
in the previous section.

Our belief in the empowering possibilities of the partnership relationship is also supported by more practical reasons for pursuing partnership.
A program's implementation will likely fail when the views of stakeholders, especially those for whom the intervention is intended, are not incorporated into the design (Peirson & Prilleltensky, 1994). Both insiders
and outsiders are needed to plan and implement a prevention program tailored to the context, one where the program is "built in" to the setting,
rather than "laid on" (Juras, Mackin, Curtis, & Foster-Fishman, 1997;
O'Neill & Trickett, 1982; Peirson & Prilleltensky, 1994). Although community members can bring insightful ideas about what might work in their
particular context, professionals can bring information about evi-
dence-based programs (Durlak & Wells, 1997) enabling community members to make informed decisions about different program options. These
typical roles notwithstanding, professionals can contribute more than
knowledge, and community members can offer more than experience.

Subsequent feelings of ownership (Altman, 1995; Cherniss, 1997;
Durlak, 1998; Kress, Cimring, & Elias, 1997; Lynch, Geller, Hunt, Galano, &

Dubas, 1998) and commitment about the program can result because stakeholders will have invested a part of themselves in the process (Gager & Elias, 1997; Peirson & Prilleltensky, 1994). In contrast, a program that is imposed from the top down can trigger indifference and even contempt and resistance (Johnson, Malone, & Hightower, 1997; Juras et al., 1997; Peirson & Prilleltensky, 1994). School administrators, teachers, parents, and students have been found to react negatively to top down changes (Johnson et al., 1997; Peirson & Prilleltensky, 1994).

How should the partnerships work? Creating the types of value-based partnerships that we propose is not easy. The challenge begins at the outset of the partnership, that is, when recruiting potential partners, and continues on throughout the life of the relationship. How do we attract members of the community, encourage them to share personal stories that inform the intervention-building process, and maintain their involvement? Cameron, Peirson, and Pancer's (1994) review of resident involvement at the seven Ontario Better Beginnings, Better Futures prevention program sites sheds light on methods that can attract prospective community members to the planning table. Their findings suggest that consultants and others from the formal sector should pay particular attention to ways in which their professional roles overtly and covertly dominate interactions with community members. For example, the authors found that the formal manner in which professionals conduct meetings, make decisions, and dominate air time during meetings can stifle resident involvement, whereas avoiding the use of professional jargon and sharing leadership responsibilities, such as chairing meetings, can facilitate community participation (Cameron et al., 1994).

Challenges for consultants. We call for consultants to abandon the role of researcher as expert (Kloos et al., 1997) and to recognize the wealth of knowledge inherent in the informal sector. When designing prevention programs, it is important that consultants and others from the formal sector share power with community members who are disadvantaged. The latter group possesses wisdom and experience, which the former group traditionally lacks. Lord and Church (1998) presented a similar view in their acknowledgement that "non-disabled professionals cannot fully understand the social world of disability" (p. 11).

Part of the challenge for consultants and other professionals is to proactively ensure the equal status of community members with whom they work (Chavis, Stucky, & Wandersman, 1983). Invitations to participate are not enough. Mandating a larger representation from the community than that of professionals has been found to facilitate the involvement of the informal sector (Cameron et al., 1994). In Ontario's Better Beginnings, Better Futures prevention program sites, there must be at least 51% community resident membership on each decision-making committee. We believe consultants should take significant strides toward building a responsive relationship with the informal sector. Researchers and professionals need to be more humble and better listeners.

Creating safe and friendly processes is vital for recruiting and maintaining the interest and participation of different stakeholders. Also, consultants and other service providers need to recognize issues of volunteer burnout and turnover over time (Pancer & Cameron, 1994). It is important not to overload or exploit parent volunteers who are not being paid for their participation, but rather to recognize and support their contributions. To address the turnover issue, which is natural and inevitable, there needs to be continuous recruitment of interested parents and students.

Illustration.   A practical example of creating a partnership for prevention can be found in Peggy's work with refugee children and families in Kitchener-Waterloo, Ontario. In this community, there is a growing number of refugee families, but little attention has been paid to addressing the needs of refugee children. Refugee parents, English as a second language teachers, counselors, health professionals, settlement workers, and other concerned community members came together to form a Community Supports Group. From its members' combined perspectives, experiences, and skills, this group is learning how to plan and develop community supports for refugee children and families.

In building its membership, the Community Supports Group has worked hard, although not always successfully, to recruit as many members as possible from communities with refugee experience. Group members from the mainstream culture make a conscious effort not to dominate discussions and to make space for the voices of those whose language and cultural background is different. Meetings are held at times and in places that are most conducive to participation from community members. Providing interpretation, transportation, and refreshments are all ways in which the group works to encourage participation in its activities.

Step 2: Clarify Values and Vision and Derive Working Principles

As we have suggested, there is a need to recognize the role of values in planning and implementing prevention programs. Whether conscious of them or not, each of us has values and beliefs that invariably affect our thoughts and actions (Prilleltensky, 1997). Our second step in value-based partnerships for effective prevention program implementation asks consultants to clarify the vision and values of the partners and to derive principles for how these partners should work together.

What is values and vision clarification? We propose that partners undergo a process of values and vision clarification. We recommend a participatory process whereby children, teachers, parents, professionals, and volunteers have a say about what values they wish to promote. All partners should bring an open mind to the process and come to a consensus about values underlying the work of the project. Shared values may be the most important factor for successful partnerships (Nelson et al., in press).

Common values serve as a reference to guide, motivate, and bond the group, thereby facilitating prevention program planning. In our experiences, we have found that the partnership values of collaboration, democratic participation, solidarity, trust, and reciprocity are vital in the creation of prevention programs, in particular, and in social cohesion, in general (Nelson et al., in press). When there is value congruence, there is potential for a good partnership and hence effective implementation (Nelson et al., in press). When there is value incongruence, partners should realize that the relationship and program implementation will be more of a struggle. Shared values can be created by devoting time and energy to extensive pre-negotiation work (Nelson et al., in press). Clarifying the *vision* entails a similar process to that of values clarification, whereby group members form a shared purpose for the partnership founded on the group's shared values (Nelson et al., in press).

What are working principles? Once an agreement on the values and vision of the partnership has been reached, the next task is to develop working principles, or the collective norms, that will govern the group. We recommend grounding those principles in the input of partners. As derivatives of the vision and values, the working principles should address how best to resolve conflict, elicit participation, and reach a consensus. We have found that, unless people learn to negotiate differences, it is not realistic to expect social harmony, let alone effective program implementation. This is why we promote partnership values, values that uphold conflict resolution and collaboration (Putnam, 1996).

Establishing clear procedures for decision making and encouraging collaborative and trusting relationships are key ingredients for successful working conditions. Well-conceived prevention programs cannot work unless the people who are supposed to implement them get along. The process of clarifying values, vision, and working principles is ongoing and fosters a sense of ownership and partnership among the players (Nelson et al., in press; Peirson & Prilleltensky, 1994; Prilleltensky et al., 1997). When individual partners are committed to the same goals and norms, a successful partnership is likely to follow (Nelson et al., in press).

Challenges for consultants.   To actualize this second step, there is a need for consultants to engage in a self-reflexive analysis of the values she or he brings to consultation practice. Dei (1996) argued that a self-reflective critique is necessary prior to engaging in transformative projects. He called for a heightened self-awareness of the ways in which we oppress and are the oppressors of others (Dei, 1996). Part of this consciousness raising should include resensitizing ourselves to the hardships experienced by people living in disadvantaged conditions (Nelson et al., in press). It is important to realize that we all have blind spots, of which we may not be aware, and assumptions about people who are disadvantaged. If such assumptions are not subjected to critical self-reflection, they might surface and interfere with our work as consultants.

On recognizing one's values, there must also be a willingness on the consultant's part to have those values challenged (Nelson et al., in press). On a personal level, when others question and criticize one's beliefs, it can lead to feelings of hurt, self-doubt, and anger. Beyond those feelings, consultants should expect to feel uncomfortable because the experience of partnering with people living in disadvantaged conditions can lead to questioning one's own privilege. Given the likelihood of discomfort, to truly engage in the partnership we propose there must be a "readiness to enter into an uncomfortable zone" (Nelson et al., in press, p. 28).

Another challenge for consultants is value incongruence between different stakeholders (Cherniss, 1993). Our experience is that this can take two different forms. One is the case in which one or more partners subscribe to values that are antithetical to those of other partners. For example, if a service provider believes that he or she is the "expert," this will undoubtedly cause problems if other partners are striving toward power sharing. Another problem is when there is a gap between the "talk" and the "walk" of the values on the part of some partners. We have experienced individuals who state that they espouse the values of the project, but their behavior is inconsistent with their words.

Both types of value incongruence mentioned previously can be overcome through opportunities for being challenged, which can lead to mutual learning and self-reflection. If, over time, value incongruence persists, the group needs to consider the participation of individual members or the viability of the present group. Perhaps different players or a different forum is needed.

Illustration.   To illustrate, a key feature of the Community Supports Group with which Peggy has been involved is the shared values that bind the group together. These include the caring and compassion that have motivated people to invest time, energy, and resources in the work; a health-oriented perspective and belief in children's resilience and capacity to heal; a commitment to community-based approaches that nurture empowerment and participation; and a conviction that individuals and groups must work together and advocate at multiple levels for a more equitable distribution of resources and opportunities for all members of the community. This group collaboratively defined its values and vision and uses them to guide the work of the group and programs that are designed to support refugee families.

The Community Supports Group did experience a serious internal crisis among group members that caused members to invest a lot of time reflecting on shared values and principles related to mutual respect and trust. This process led to a resolution of the issues, created a safe environment for those who had felt threatened, and enhanced group members' relationships and their capacity to work together.

Step 3: Identify and Merge the Strengths of Different Approaches and Partners

What are the different approaches?   The third step in the development of value-based partnerships is to identify the strengths of different approaches and partners and to creatively merge the different strengths. In the first step, we identified the different stakeholder groups who need to be involved in value-based partnerships for prevention. It is important for consultants to recognize that each partner has strengths and brings something valuable to the planning and implementation process. This strengths-based focus has long been a key concept of community psychology (Rappaport, 1977). As planning group members first meet and get to know one another, they can engage in mapping the assets of group members and of the community (McKnight, 1995). Focusing on strengths can energize the group and community for action.

It is also important for consultants to recognize that different stakeholders often work from different approaches and different bases of knowledge. Prevention researchers typically work from a deductive and nomothetic approach that is associated with formal research knowledge. The deductive and nomothetic perspective is a rational, empirical approach to implementing programs based on traditional notions of the scientific method.

On the other hand, service providers and community members typically work from an inductive and experiential approach, which is associated with experiential knowledge. This approach focuses explicitly on the politics and interpersonal relationships that are inherent in social research and intervention. Moreover, this approach asserts that the voices of people for whom an intervention is developed should be at the forefront of the change process because citizens have essential information and experience to contribute to such interventions, as well as a democratic right to self-determination.

It is important for consultants to recognize that different approaches and types of knowledge are valuable and important for prevention program implementation. Recently, the dominance of the deductive and nomothetic approach has been challenged on the grounds that it ignores the value-laden and political nature of most human problems (Lincoln & Guba, 1985). This does not mean that this approach is not useful, but that it should be balanced with the inductive and experiential approach by including and listening to the voices of the community.

Why should we merge different approaches?   Our belief is that the inductive and experiential and deductive and nomothetic approaches are complementary, rather than contradictory, and that they need to be bridged in prevention program implementation. It is not enough to have impeccable theoretical formulations for a problem or program if they are not accepted or understood by people and do not reflect the people's realities (Bowden, 1997; Chambliss, 1996).

Partnerships provide an ideal forum for melding these two perspectives, given that the values of conflict resolution and collaboration are fundamental to the relationship (Putnam, 1996). Our experiences as prevention program planners have taught us that disagreements about how to intervene are an inevitable part of the partnership. However, as members negotiate past differences and synthesize ideas about implementation, the bonds between partners can be reinforced. Moreover, individual commitment to the partnership relationship, and to the implementation project, can also be strengthened (Gager & Elias, 1997; Peirson & Prilleltensky, 1994).

Challenges for consultants.   In practice, combining the deductive and nomothetic and inductive and experiential approaches to program implementation is challenging. For consultants, the challenge lies in their ability to facilitate the involvement of members from both the formal and informal sectors (Cameron et al., 1994). Community members are likely unaccustomed to sharing their stories to inform program implementation. Having traditionally been overlooked in the planning process, eliciting their participation can be difficult. Feelings of self-doubt about one's knowledge and skills, as well as a mistrust for the partnership process, are likely to hinder involvement (Cameron et al., 1994; Nelson et al., 1999). Moreover, Cameron et al. noted that most professionals are not trained in ways to effectively involve residents. This is likely due to the traditionally individualistic, expert role of consultants.

To begin to move past the discomfort, there is a need to develop a safe climate (Nelson et al., in press). Much attention must be spent on ensuring that all participants are comfortable, feeling accepted and valued (Kloos et al., 1997; Nelson et al., 1999; Prilleltensky et al., 1997). Consultants will need to have patience (Nelson et al., in press): As with any relationship, developing a level of trust takes time (Perkins & Wandersman, 1990). A consultant cannot overestimate the importance of time when developing the partnership (Juras et al., 1997; Kloos et al., 1997; Nelson et al., in press) because the rapport among the consultant, prospective service users, and other stakeholders is the foundation for dialogue.

Consultants need to value the experiential knowledge of community members and service providers from the setting. The approaches and knowledge bases of professionals and disadvantaged citizens are like different worlds. Bridging these two worlds or cultures is quite a formidable challenge. We have found that language can be a barrier to such bridging. Researchers and professionals need to be wary of research and professional jargon and learn to speak in more easily understood terms. Our experience is that in bridging this gap, it is important both to find common ground and to understand and respect differences (Lord & Church, 1998). One helpful factor in this process is the location and inclusion of *boundary spanners* (i.e., people who have experience in, and can understand, both worlds; Bond & Keys, 1993). Another helpful factor is to have partners skilled in conflict resolution (Nelson et al., in press).

Illustration.   In the formative meetings of Peggy's involvement with different stakeholders concerned with refugee children, a capacity-oriented skills and resources inventory of group members was taken. A nominal group process was then used to identify and set priorities for the group's objectives in a participatory and democratic fashion. This process empowered the group by documenting its collective wealth of knowledge and experience. It also elicited and validated the various kinds of resources that each person could contribute and established an ethic of mutual respect that group members have worked hard to promote.

A valuable process of mutual learning occurred within the group as different members complemented each other's theoretical and practical knowledge. Several members with clinical and academic backgrounds shared their knowledge of the concepts of risk and protective factors as related to children and trauma. Settlement workers and refugee members enhanced and expanded on this with real life examples of what they had experienced or observed in refugee children. English as a second language teachers were identified as pivotal in building bridges within and among the school, refugee families, and the larger community. The group was extremely fortunate to have several boundary spanners, who combined refugee and psychology, teacher and refugee, and immigrant and community psychology experience. The work of the Community Supports Group illustrates the importance of both the deductive and nomothetic and inductive and experiential aspects of planning.

Step 4: Define the Problem Collaboratively

For the fourth step in developing value-based partnerships for effective prevention program implementation, we recommend that stakeholders from the formal and informal sectors define the focal problem together, combining deductive and nomothetic and inductive and experiential approaches. The deductive and nomothetic approach includes attention to risk and protective factors and how they operate in a multi-level, ecological context on the focal problem. Cowen (1980) referred to this as the *generative base* of prevention, and Reiss and Price (1996) spoke of *life span human development* to capture this idea. Bloom (1984) asserted that in establishing the generative base of a social problem, one first decides on the focus of the preventive intervention and then constructs a model of how the problem develops. This involves defining the problem and assessing how widespread the problem is in a community.

The most popular, current theoretical approach for understanding the problems of children and youth involves an examination of the risk and protective factors that may influence the problem of concern (Bogenschneider, 1996; Rae-Grant, 1994). Risk factors are those that are associated with an increased likelihood of the problem, whereas protective factors are those that enhance an individual's ability to cope with risk factors, thus reducing the likelihood of the problem (Rutter, 1987).

Related to the risk and protective factors framework is the ecological perspective. Bronfenbrenner (1986) asserted that a child is embedded within a number of nested and interdependent systems, including the microsystem (e.g., the family), mesosystems (e.g., schools, neighborhoods), and macrosystems (e.g., culture, media). Several writers have examined a variety of child and youth problems, such as delinquency and substance abuse, in terms of risk and protective factors at the child, family, and community levels of analysis (Hawkins, Catalano, & Miller, 1992; Rae-Grant, 1994; Yoshikawa, 1994).

However, in framing the problem for a preventive intervention, it is not enough for researchers to have a conceptual analysis based on the best information in the research literature. The inductive and experiential perspective reminds us that there must also be an understanding of, and an active engagement with, the school and/or community in which the preventive intervention is to be implemented (Bogenschneider, 1996; Peirson & Prilleltensky, 1994; Reiss & Price, 1996). A local planning committee, consisting of different stakeholders, can formulate the problem for the intervention. This approach has been successfully used in the development of a mentoring program in a high school (Peirson & Prilleltensky, 1994) and in the formulation of proposals for multi-component, community-based prevention programs in Ontario, known as Better Beginnings, Better Futures (Pancer & Cameron, 1994).

It is important for the most disadvantaged stakeholder group to have a voice in defining the group's problems and strengths. In the Better Beginnings program sites, Pancer and Cameron (1994) found that parents with a low income both benefited from and contributed through their participation. Such a process builds ownership and the commitment of stakeholders and brings resources from the host setting to the planning and implementation process, factors that have been found to be associated with effective prevention program implementation (Gager & Elias, 1997; Peirson & Prilleltensky, 1994).

One of the benefits of involving community members in a community needs assessment is that they are very knowledgeable about their community's strengths, resources, and capacities on which any proposed intervention can build (McKnight, 1995). They are, in addition, quite rightly sensitive to having their communities labeled in terms of problems or deficits.

Challenges for consultants.   Combining   the   two   approaches achieves a more thorough understanding of the focal problem and strengths than does conventional consultation. Like the medical model, traditional consultants work alone to assess and diagnose the setting *for* its members. In contrast, our proposal involves working *with* community members for a problem definition that builds a comprehensive understanding of the problem. Our proposal is based on a collaborative process where lived experience informs research, just as research informs people's understanding of the issues. The main challenge for consultants trying to implement this step is for them to engage in a collaborative process.

Another challenge for consultants is to educate community members about the risk and protective factor framework at multiple ecological levels of analysis. This model needs to be described in plain language using examples that are relevant to community members. Community members can then understand its value as a tool and use it to educate consultants about the most salient risks and protective factors in their communities. Thus, the process is one of mutual learning between the consultant and the community.

Illustration.   Isaac has collaborated with a group of Latin American refugee families in Kitchener-Waterloo, Ontario, to improve the educational and personal opportunities of their children. Having grown up in Argentina and having experienced migration twice in his life, Isaac felt close to the community and its challenges. The families lived in a cooperative housing with about 80 units, and Latin American families occupied about one fourth of them. Parents had been concerned about the schools' responsiveness to their children's needs and came together to form the Latin American Educational Group.

To determine the children's needs, Isaac and the group conducted a needs and resources assessment. With collaboration from community leaders, they constructed an interview guide inquiring about risk and protective factors facing the children and families in this refugee community. Isaac trained community members in interviewing and focus group facilitation. Several parents helped with the research, including the analysis and interpretation. The findings were conceptualized at various levels of analysis. Risk, protective factors, and recommendations were all discussed at the levels of child, family, school, and community (Prilleltensky, 1993).

Two of the central problems that were identified were the need to prevent smoking and the need to promote the Spanish language skills of children. The work of this group illustrates the type of collaborative approach to problem definition and needs and resources assessment that we are proposing.

Step 5: Develop the Prevention Program Collaboratively

The fifth step maintains that the prevention program should be developed collaboratively. The appropriateness of a solution depends on participatory decision making with those most vulnerable to the focal problem. We again argue that the prevention program should be based on a synthesis of the deductive and nomothetic and inductive and experiential approaches.

The deductive and nomothetic approach encourages planners to review theoretical formulations about prevention models and the qualities of effective prevention programs. Three types of prevention have been delineated in the literature: (a) proactive universal prevention (which is for everyone), (b) proactive high-risk prevention (which is for groups that are high-risk for developing a problem), and (c) reactive interventions (which treat problems in their early stages; Nelson, Laurendeau, Chamberland, & Peirson, 1999, Nelson, Prilleltensky, & Peters, 1999). Some writers are against subsuming reactive efforts under the larger *prevention umbrella*, maintaining that such efforts are really treatment services (Durlak, 1997; Goldston, 1986). Nonetheless, research shows that early intervention to reduce the negative effects of an existing problem is worthwhile because the likelihood of long-term maladjustment is diminished if milder problems are prevented from getting worse (Durlak & Wells, 1998).

Recent frameworks of preventive intervention draw from the generative base of the focal problem to formulate strategies that reduce risks and reinforce the presence of protective factors. It is through multi-component interventions that address the risk and protective factors at the micro, meso, and macrosystems that a child's development is best protected and promoted (Rae-Grant, 1994). Consistent with an ecological perspective, this multiple-level understanding of preventive interventions also calls planners to identify resources in the focal and related systems that facilitate intervention implementation. Peirson (1993) outlined two such resources. The term *hardware* describes the tangible resources needed to properly implement and sustain changes to a setting. People, funding, material resources, staff training, and pilot programs are some of the facilitative factors befitting the hardware classification (Durlak, 1998; Lynch et al., 1998; Peirson, 1993). *Software* refers to the intangible factors that ease implementation, such as a long-term approach to the change process. Although previous research serves as an informative foundation from which to build an intervention, an understanding of the present context is still necessary. The inductive and experiential perspective fulfills this need.

The inductive and experiential approach to intervention is rooted in the strengths and views of those who are disadvantaged and in cultivating a respectful collaboration with them. Exploring what residents believe to be helpful in their context in terms of prevention and promotion of wellness is central to forming relationships and benefitting from capacities. Using grounded theory (Peirson & Prilleltensky, 1994), planners should explore people's hopes for the intervention and how they feel their needs can be best met:

> For programs and change to be considered successful, community members must come to see them as their changes. However, for stakeholders to take ownership and believe a program/change is theirs, they must be able to recognize in it some of themselves: their needs, their beliefs, their ideas. (Peirson & Prilleltensky, 1994, p. 137)

Community residents must be involved in planning. The greater the community involvement, the more likely the community will be to support the intervention. In turn, an enhanced sense of ownership over the school or community program can result, and institutionalization of the prevention program is likely (Altman, 1995; Cherniss, 1997; Durlak, 1998; Kress et al., 1997; Lynch et al., 1998).

Fullan (1992) asserted that implementation of school innovation is enhanced when stakeholders agree on the need for change and the relevance of the intervention for the school. We believe that reaching an agreement about a setting's needs, and an intervention's relevance, require both the inductive and experiential and deductive and nomothetic perspectives. Whereas the deductive and nomothetic probes the theoretical underpinnings that have informed past interventions about the focal problem, the inductive and experiential approach reveals the present concerns and hopes stakeholders have about dealing with the issue. In the end, a comprehensive understanding of the necessary supports can, ideally, be attained.

Challenges for consultants.   The main challenge for consultants at the fifth step of our proposed implementation is to help the group reconcile differences and build a consensus about a prevention program approach. Whereas deductively oriented partners are likely to purport replicating programs that have been evaluated and proven effective in other settings, inductively oriented partners are more inclined to implement innovative preventive supports. Moreover, there are often conflicting ideas about whether an intervention should strive for immediate or long-term benefits.

We have found that achieving short-term goals builds confidence among partners and trust in others affected by the intervention. While partners come to believe in the effectiveness of the partnership relationship, members of the setting can become more receptive to future changes having witnessed previous success (Peirson & Prilleltensky, 1994). Achieving short-term goals prepares partners and the setting to attain goals that require more intense planning, commitment, and time. These debates of replication versus innovation and short- versus long-term goals are issues that consultants will likely need to mediate with others in the partnership.

Illustration.   Isaac's work with the Latin American community led to several different prevention and promotion programs. Multiple needs called for multiple interventions at various levels and with various players. At the level of the child, there was a need to maintain cultural heritage. This prompted the creation of a Spanish school run by parent volunteers. At the family level, there was a need for parenting courses, which were coordinated by local facilitators. At the school level, advocacy was needed to help educators understand the unique circumstances of refugee children from Latin America. This led to presentations and meetings with school board officials.

At the level of the community, smoking prevention was seen as a priority. With government funding, a local initiative was launched to prevent smoking in children and youth. This program was not limited to skills, but incorporated a community action component. Children made presentations at city hall concerning the ill effects of smoking and displayed antismoking art in a shopping center.

Step Six: Research and Evaluate Collaboratively

The final step in developing value-based partnership for effective implementation asks consultants to partner with program participants, other professionals, and community members in researching and evaluating the implementation of the prevention program. Once again, we believe that research and evaluation should blend the deductive and nomothetic and inductive and experiential perspectives. The deductive and nomothetic approach includes various process and outcome measures related to program implementation, whereas the inductive and experiential approach is used to gather qualitative data regarding the implementation process as perceived by different stakeholders.

We propose an evaluation of each of the six steps. A deductively oriented evaluation measures the extent to which each step is successfully completed, whereas an inductively oriented evaluation focuses more on the process behind fulfilling each task; that is, how do partners experience the partnership relationship? For example, a deductively oriented evaluation of step five (i.e., develop and implement a prevention program) investigates the extent to which the program is implemented as planned (Durlak, 1998). Quantitative measures of program fidelity can be used for this approach. An inductively oriented evaluation investigates how partners feel about the evaluation process. Issues of resident participation, personal empowerment, and social climate are addressed by using qualitative interviews and observations more in line with inductive and experiential data-gathering tools. An excellent example of how these two approaches can be combined in the study of prevention programs for children is that of Better Beginnings, Better Futures (Peters, 1994).

We believe it is important that both approaches be used in a collaborative, participatory manner. Having research steering committees composed of community members and service providers to guide each step of the research process is one way to promote collaborative research, using either quantitative or qualitative methods (Nelson et al., 1998).

Challenges for consultants.   The final challenge for educational and psychological consultants is to facilitate the sharing of the evaluation process between formal and informal sectors. To do so, partnership resources need to be distributed in a manner that enables all stakeholders to take part in the evaluation (Nelson et al,. 1998). Educating and training partners who are unfamiliar with research methods is one way of equalizing the participation between the two sectors. Hiring people who are economically disadvantaged from the host community as research assistants is another viable method.

Illustration.   Isaac's work with the Latin American community illustrates the type of participatory research related to prevention program implementation that we are advocating. Throughout the 6 years the various projects were in operation, the group conducted formal and informal evaluations to see how people got along and how effective the programs were. Isaac and members of the steering committee hired and trained research assistants to gather data for the evaluations. For example, a quantitative, outcome evaluation with a comparison group of the smoking prevention program was conducted. As well, qualitative data were collected from children, parents, and project workers about the implementation of the smoking prevention program.

CONCLUSION

In this article, we highlighted the importance of values and partnerships for effective prevention program implementation. Following from these concepts, we outlined six steps in the planning and implementation process that we believe are helpful guidelines for educational and psychological consultants who are interested in developing school and community prevention programs. For each step, we have identified some key tasks, processes, and challenges for consultants.

Based on our reading of the prevention literature, we found that seldom is there a mention of the first three steps (creating partnerships, clarifying values and vision and deriving working principles, and identifying and merging the strengths of different approaches and stakeholders). These steps are central to our conceptualization of effective implementation. We believe that effective prevention programs need to be grounded in consensually agreed on values and solid partnership relationships among consultants, human service providers, and people for whom the intervention is designed that acknowledge and build upon one another's strengths. This is the essence of the first three steps.

Again, based on our reading of the prevention literature, we found that most consultants ignore the first three steps, beginning instead with the last three (defining the focal problem, developing a prevention program, and researching and evaluating the program). That is, consultants immediately dive into the task of analyzing the problem, creating a solution, and evaluating the solution. Moreover, these steps are typically done by researchers and human service providers, with those who are to be the recipients of the intervention being ignored in this process. Our belief is that parents, students, and other community members should be integrally and meaningfully involved in these latter three steps.

We acknowledge that some researchers and consultants may follow the path that we have outlined in the previous paragraphs. However, if they are behaving in a more value-based, partnership-oriented, collaborative manner, then they are not writing about it. For the reasons that we have outlined throughout this article, we urge consultants to follow the suggested guidelines and to report, in the prevention literature, their experiences.

REFERENCES

Altman, D. (1995). Sustaining interventions in community settings: On the relationship between researchers and communities. *Health Psychology, 14,* 526–536.

Bloom, B. L. (1984). *Community mental health* (2nd ed.). Monterey, CA: Brooks/Cole.

Bogenschneider, K. (1996). An ecological risk/protective theory for building prevention programs, policies, and community capacity to support youth. *Family Relations, 45,* 127–138.

Bond, M. A., & Keys, C. B. (1993). Empowerment, diversity, and collaboration: Promoting synergy on community boards. *American Journal of Community Psychology, 21,* 37–57.

Bowden, P. (1997). *Caring: Gender-sensitive ethics.* London: Routledge & Kegan Paul.

Bronfenbrenner, U. (1986). Ecology of the family as a context for human development: Research perspectives. *Developmental Psychology, 22,* 723–742.

Cameron, G., Peirson, L., & Pancer, M. (1994). Resident participation in the Better Beginnings, Better Futures prevention project: Part II—Factors that facilitate and hinder involvement. *Canadian Journal of Community Mental Health, 13,* 213–228.

Chambliss, D. (1996). *Beyond caring: Hospitals, nurses, and the social organization of ethics.* Chicago: University of Chicago Press.

Chavis, D., M., Stucky, P. E., & Wandersman, A. (1983). Returning basic research to the community: A relationship between scientist and citizen. *American Psychologist, 28,* 424–434.

Cherniss, C. (1993). Pre-entry issues revisited. In R. T. Golembiewski (Ed.), *Handbook of organizational consultation* (pp. 113–118). New York: Marcel Dekker.

Cherniss, C. (1997). Teacher empowerment, consultation and the creation of new programs in school. *Journal of Educational and Psychological Consultation, 8,* 135–152.

Cowen, E. L. (1980). The wooing of primary prevention. *American Journal of Community Psychology, 8,* 258–284.

Dei, G. J. S. (1996). *Anti-racism education: Theory and practice.* Halifax, Nova Scotias, Canada: Fernwook.

Dimock, H. G. (1992). *Intervention and empowerment: Helping organizations to change.* North York, Ontario, Cananda: Captus Press.

Durlak, J. A. (1997). *Successful prevention programs for children and adolescents.* New York: Plenum.

Durlak, J. A. (1998). Why program implementation is important. *Journal of Prevention and Intervention in the Community, 17,* 5–18.

Durlak, J. A., & Wells, A. M. (1997). Primary prevention mental health programs for children and adolescents: A meta-analytic review. *American Journal of Community Psychology, 25,* 145–150.

Durlak, J. A., & Wells, A. M. (1998). Evaluation of indicated preventive intervention (secondary prevention) mental health programs for children and adolescents. *American Journal of Community Psychology, 26,* 775–802.

Fullan, M. (1992). *Successful school improvement: The implementation perspective and beyond.* Buckingham, England: Open University Press.

Gager, P. J., & Elias, M. J. (1997). Implementing prevention programs in high-risk environments: Application of the resiliency paradigm. *American Journal of Orthopsychiatry, 67,* 363–373.

Goldston, S. E. (1986). Primary prevention: Historical perspectives and a blueprint for action. *American Psychologist, 46,* 642–648.

Hawkins, J. D., Catalano, R. F., & Miller, J. Y. (1992). Risk and protective factors for alcohol and other drug problems in adolescence and early childhood: Implications for substance abuse prevention. *Psychological Bulletin, 112,* 64–105.

Johnson, D. B., Malone, P. J., & Hightower, A. D. (1997). Barriers to primary prevention efforts in the schools: Are we the biggest obstacle to the transfer of knowledge? *Applied and Preventive Psychology, 6,* 81–90.

Juras, J., Mackin, J. R., Curtis, S. E., & Foster-Fishman P. G. (1997). Key concepts of community psychology: Implications for consulting in education and human services settings. *Journal of Educational and Psychological Consultation, 8,* 111–134.

Kekes, J. (1993). *The morality of pluralism.* Princeton, NJ: Princeton University Press.

Kloos, B., McCoy, J., Stewart, E., Thomas, E. R., Wiley, A., Good, T. L., Hunt, G. D., Moore, T., & Rappaport, J. (1997). Bridging the gap: A community-based, open-systems approach to school and neighborhood consultation. *Journal of Educational and Psychological Consultation, 8,* 175–196.

Kress, J. S., Cimring, B. R., & Elias, M. J. (1997). Community psychology consultation and the transition to institutional ownership and operation of intervention. *Journal of Educational and Psychological Consultation, 8,* 231–253.

Lord, J., & Church, K. (1998). Beyond "partnership shock": Getting to "yes," living with "no." *Canadian Journal of Rehabilitation, 12,* 113–121.

Lincoln, Y. S., & Guba, E. (1985). *Naturalistic inquiry.* Beverly Hills, CA: Sage.

Lynch, K. B., Geller, S. R., Hunt, D. R., Galano, J., & Dubas, J. S. (1998). Successful program development using implementation evaluation. *Journal of Prevention and Intervention in the Community, 17,* 51–64.

MacGillivary, H., & Nelson, G. (1998). Partnership in mental health: What it is and how to do it. *Canadian Journal of Rehabilitation, 12,* 71–83.

Mayton, D. M., Ball-Rokeach, S. J., & Loges, W. E. (1994). Human values and social issues: An introduction. *Journal of Social Issues, 50*(4), 1–8.

McKnight, J. (1995). *The careless society: Community and its counterfeits.* New York: Basic Books.

Narayan, J. (1999, March). *Building for community.* Keynote address to the Kitchener Downtown Inter-Community Health Centre, Kitchener, Ontario.

Nelson, G., Laurendeau, M. -C., Chamberland, C., & Peirson, L. (1999). A review and analysis of programs to promote family wellness and prevent the maltreatment of pre-school and school-aged children. In I. Prilleltensky, G. Nelson, & L. Peirson (Eds.), *Promoting family wellness and preventing child maltreatment* (pp. 221–287). Final report to Social Development Partnerships, Human Resources Development Canada. Waterloo, Ontario, Canada: Social Development Partnerships, Human Resources Development Canada.

Nelson, G., Ochocka, J., Griffin, K., & Lord, J. (1998). "Nothing about me, without me": Participatory action research with self-help/mutual aid organizations for psychiatric consumer/survivors. *American Journal of Community Psychology, 26,* 881–912.

Nelson, G., Prilleltensky, I., & MacGillivary, H. (in press). Building value-based partnerships: Toward solidarity with oppressed groups. *American Journal of Community Psychology.*

Nelson, G., Prilleltensky, I., & Peters, R. D. (1999). Prevention and mental health promotion in the community. In W. Marshall & P. Firestone (Eds.), *Abnormal psychology* (pp. 461–478. Scarborough, Ontario, Canada: Prentice Hall.

O'Neill, P., & Trickett, E. J. (1982). *Community consultation.* San Francisco: Jossey-Bass.

Pancer, S. M., & Cameron, G. (1994). Resident participation in the Better Beginnings, Better Futures prevention project: Part I—The impacts of involvement. *Canadian Journal of Community Mental Health, 13,* 197–211.

Peirson, L. (1993). *The development of a preventive peer mentoring program for students: Grounded theory at work.* Unpublished master's thesis, Wilfrid Laurier University, Waterloo, Ontario, Canada.

Peirson, L., & Prilleltensky, I. (1994). Understanding school change to facilitate prevention: A study of change in a secondary school. *Canadian Journal of Community Mental Health, 13,* 127–144.

Perkins, D. D., & Wandersman, A. (1990). "You'll have to work to overcome our suspicions": The benefits and pitfalls of research with community organizations. *Social Policy, 20,* 32–41.

Peters, R. D. (1994). Better Beginnings, Better Futures: A community-based approach to primary prevention. *Canadian Journal of Community Mental Health, 13,* 183–188.

Powell, B., & Nelson, G. (1997). The cultivation of neighbourhood centers: A lifecycle model. *Journal for the Community Development Society, 28,* 25–42.

Prilleltensky, I. (1993). The immigration experience of Latin-American families: Research and action on perceived risk and protective factors. *Canadian Journal of Community Mental Health, 12,* 101–116.

Prilleltensky, I. (1997). Values, assumptions, and practices: Assessing the moral implications of psychological discourse and action. *American Psychologist, 47,* 517–535.

Prilleltensky, I., & Nelson, G. (1997). Community psychology: Reclaiming social justice. In D. Fox & I. Prilleltensky (Eds.), *Critical psychology: An introduction* (pp. 166–184). London: Sage.

Prilleltensky, I., Peirson, L., & Nelson, G. (1997). The application of community psychology values and guiding concepts to school consultation. *Journal of Educational and Psychological Consultation, 8,* 153–173.

Putnam, R. W. (1996). Creating reflective dialogue. In S. Toulmin & B. Gustavsen (Eds.), *Beyond theory: Changing organizations through participation* (pp. 41–52). Philadelphia: John Benjamins North America.

Rae-Grant, N. I. (1994). Preventive interventions for children and adolescents: Where are we now and how far have we come? *Canadian Journal of Community Mental Health, 13,* 17–36.

Rappaport, J. (1977). *Community psychology: Values, research, and action.* New York: Holt, Rinehart & Winston.

Reiss, D., & Price, R. H. (1996). National research agenda for prevention research: The National Institute of Mental Health Report. *American Psychologist, 51,* 1109–1115.

Rutter, M. (1987). Psychosocial resilience and protective mechanisms. *American Journal of Orthopsychiatry, 57,* 316–331.

Schorr, L. B. (1997). *Common purpose: Strengthening families and neighborhoods to rebuild America.* New York: Anchor.

Schwartz, S. H. (1994). Are there universal aspects in the structure and contents of human values? *Journal of Social Issues, 50*(4), 19–46.

Yoshikawa, H. (1994). Prevention as cumulative protection: Effects of early family support and education on chronic delinquency and its risks. *Psychological Bulletin, 115,* 28–54.

Geoffrey Nelson is Professor of Psychology and Director of the Master of Arts Program in Community Psychology at Wilfrid Laurier University. He has served as Senior Editor of the *Canadian Journal of Community Mental Health* and Chair of the Community Psychology Section of the Canadian Psychological Association. Some of his research and writing have focused on community- and school-based prevention programs for children and families.

Jeannette L. Amio completed her master of arts in the Community Psychology Program at Wilfrid Laurier University. She is currently a Doctor of Educational Psychology at the Ontario Institute for Studies in Education, University of Toronto. Her research interests include full-service schools and the development, implementation, and evaluation of preventive school supports for newcomer children and their families.

Isaac Prilleltensky was Associate Professor of Psychology at Wilfrid Laurier University, and is currently Professor of Psychology at Victoria University, Melbourne, Australia. He is the author of *The Morals and Politics of Psychology: Psychological Discourse and the Status Quo* (1994, State University of New York Press) and Co-Editor, with Dennis Fox, of *Critical Psychology* (1997, Sage). Isaac is interested in the promotion of value-based practice and interventions in community mental health and believes that social justice is a key value in the prevention of psychological problems and in the promotion of personal and collective wellness.

Peggy Nickels completed the Master of Arts Program in Community Psychology at Wilfrid Laurier University and is a longtime worker in the fields of community and international development. She is currently the Program Coordinator of the Kitchener Downtown Inter-Community Health Centre Project. The focus of her work is community-based social change, primarily in the areas of health, the environment, immigrant and refugee issues, and social justice.

JOURNAL OF EDUCATIONAL AND PSYCHOLOGICAL CONSULTATION, 11(1), 147–172

Building an Intervention: A Theoretical and Practical Infrastructure for Planning, Implementing, and Evaluating a Metropolitan-Wide School-To-Career Initiative

Charles T. Diebold
University of Missouri–Kansas City

Ginny Miller
The Learning Exchange

Leah K. Gensheimer
University of Missouri–Kansas City

Elaine Mondschein and Harold Ohmart
The Learning Exchange

A blueprint for planning, implementing, and evaluating (PIE) an intervention is presented against the backdrop of a construction analogy. Emphasized is the interplay among theory, research, and practice throughout the PIE process, and operationalized are key terms to guide planners in their own PIE process.

Correspondence should be addressed to Charles T. Diebold, Department of Psychology, University of Missouri-Kansas City, 5100 Rockhill Road, Kansas City, MO 64110. E-mail: cdiebold@cctr.umkc.edu

Correspondence specific to School-To-Career should be addressed to Ginny Miller, The Learning Exchange, 3132 Pennsylvania, Kansas City, MO 64111. E-mail: vmiller@lx.org or visit www.lx.org

A model of ecological innovation and change, the assimmodation innovation model, is introduced to explain the process associated with the implementation and adoption of an innovation and to inform a containment × change and growth model of social action and human development. Illustrated is Kansas City's Business/Education Expectations (BE^2): School-To-Career Partnership, a comprehensive, metropolitan-wide, multiple-county school reform initiative that developed out of the *School-to-Work Opportunities Act of 1994* that seeks a pedagogy and curriculum that enhances student achievement through authentic, contextual, real world thinking and experience.

Interventions are not born; they are made. Some are constructed better than others, as the three little pigs discovered. In a way, this article is a do-it-yourself guide to building a sound intervention, one that is resistant to the huffs and puffs that have blown down so many throughout the history of social reforms and innovations. It is not a simple guide. Social issues and conditions are not simple. Typically, social interventions intend to create change. This article, an intervention in its own way, intends to change the landscape of ill-planned "pop-up programs" that have become so prevalent and have cooled the public confidence toward any intervention's ability to "make a difference." Our how-to is versatile. For context and color we present it relative to a comprehensive school-to-career initiative.

The School-To-Work Opportunities Act of 1994 (1994) established a national framework for the collaborative development of educational and career systems. The School-To-Career (STC) system in the Kansas City metropolitan region is administered by the Business/Education Expectations (BE²):School-To-Career Partnership (The Partnership), which is one of a variety of school reform initiatives facilitated by The Learning Exchange, a national center for educational consulting, training, and research.

The Partnership, which officially formed in December 1994, is now one of the nation's largest, and one of only a handful to reach across state lines. The Partnership region includes over 240,000 students in more than 48 school districts, of which 35 were directly involved in the Partnership in 1999. This article represents The Partnership's STC Initiative (the Initiative), which, when forced into a paragraph, has been described as follows:

> School-To-Career makes learning more relevant and meaningful for kids. It's about helping students know what they are learning, why they are learning it and how they will use it. School-To-Career is an approach to learning that acknowledges that kids learn best when they learn by doing. It is based on the idea that learning happens in many places and with many people. Parents, business persons and community organizations help kids learn by working with schools and providing opportunities for kids to learn in real world settings outside of school. [BE^2: School-To-Career Partnership (BE^2: STCP), 1998c, p. 6].

It is our hope that our examples of the complex interplay between theory and practice at individual, organizational, and system strata transcend our context and coalesce into a coherent heuristic.

This article is organized under the headings of *planning, implementing, and evaluating* (PIE)—although it would be a mistake to infer that these are discrete functions or strictly linear in their manifestation—and concludes with a summary of implications for consultation and intervention development. Planning involves the establishment of a purpose as realized through theoretical and empirical grounding, needs assessment, and articulation of policy. Implementing involves constructing the organizational and intervention infrastructure, both with attention to assimilation and accommodation and multi-strata strategies. Evaluating involves calibration and correction as these relate to establishing a logic model and selecting an evaluation philosophy, design, and methodology and analyzing and drawing conclusions from data.

Planning, implementing, and evaluating are interconnected. The end state of an intervention is not a "mission accomplished" closure, but a continuous, cyclical process.

PLANNING

Before the first floor of a skyscraper is evident, years of planning have been invested in the project, for example, architectural prints are rendered, the site is surveyed, core samples of the foundational soil are analyzed, applicable building codes are identified, engineering blueprints are detailed, the terrain is shaped, support piers are drilled to bedrock, and perimeter footings of steel-reinforced concrete are cast below the heaving peril of the frost line. This is as it should be. Yet, social reform projects are often expected to emerge spontaneously in toto at the penthouse, so to speak.

There simply is no substitute for planning. Findings from a summer program component of the Initiative reinforced this fact (Diebold, 1998b). The component engaged 94 middle and high school students, 7 educators, and 43 employers in a 6-week program of work-based experiences and school-based curricula enrichment. Educators and employers were asked to assess the planning and the implementation phases of the program. Two types of recommendations for planning-phase improvement were predominately offered: (a) more communication and organization and (b) to start planning earlier. Moreover, the suggestion for implementation-phase improvement that was most frequently offered was to "improve the planning and preparation process" (Diebold, 1998b, p. 8), specifically to "have more planning meetings throughout the year by everyone involved including ... staff, students, teachers, etc." (Diebold, 1998b, p. 8).

Systematic planning requires theoretical and empirical grounding, needs assessment, and articulation of policy.

Theoretical and Empirical Grounding

In general, after identifying a social issue or condition, intervention planners must deliberately ground PIE in the bedrock of theoretical and empirical wisdom. Theory is "an abstraction from practice, [and] the principle from which practice proceeds" (Runes, 1983, p. 333). Thus, theory and practice are codetermined. Unfortunately, interventions too often are planned, implemented, and evaluated without regard to the bedrock upon which they are built. Without theory we cannot understand the intervention (Price, 1987). Moreover, we cannot properly plan, implement, or evaluate one. The Partnership specifically grounded itself in theories of pedagogy, learning, and human and community development.

The Partnership also conducted an extensive empirical search of "best practices" engaged in by other STC initiatives throughout the country (e.g., Austin; Boston; Fort Worth; Grand Rapids; Green Bay; Louisville; Milwaukee; North Clackamas, Oregon; Philadelphia; Sacramento; and Tulsa). The Partnership also sought expertise and consultation from national STC technical assistance centers (e.g., Center for Career and Work-Related Education, Institute for Workforce Education, Jobs for the Future, National Alliance of Business, National Employer Leadership Council, National School-to-Work Office, New Ways Workers, School & Main, and Vision Link). The information obtained allowed The Partnership to capitalize on the successes of others; to adapt the wheel rather than reinvent it.

Additionally, relevant theories and practices that emerge from needs assessment and articulation of policy should also be taken into deliberate account.

Needs Assessment

Rossi and Freeman (1993) stated that "qualitative procedures can be especially effective in determining the *nature* of the need; [while] quantitative procedures are essential in determining the *extent* of the need" (p. 84). In 1995, The Partnership conducted both. In our construction analogy, if the enabling legislation (*School-To-Work Opportunities Act of 1994*, 1994) was the architectural rendering, then needs assessment was the survey of the site. Qualitatively, a catalog of existing metropolitan-area school, community, and business programs that fell within a broad definition of STC activities was compiled. This not only illuminated the who, what, and where of what was, but also of what was not–both of which informed later developments, for example, partnership assemblage and implementation targets.

Furthermore, core samples of the foundational soil were conducted by way of focus groups of key stakeholders, including students, parents, teachers, employers, and community-based organizations. These efforts provided insight into stakeholder expectations and potential barriers. For example, one expectation was that "teacher training and opportunities for professional development are critically needed and the responsibility for meeting these needs should be shared between schools providing in-service training and employers providing industry and technical expertise" (Kansas City Regional School-To-Career Partnership, 1995, p. 4). A potential barrier was that "some businesses may view STC activities as solely a 'civic duty' and believe that STC-style pedagogy and curricula are the school system's responsibility, not theirs" (BE[2]:STCP of Kansas City, 1996, p. 6).

A sense of the *extent* of need was discerned from the identification of human, material, and fiscal resources, and an examination of social and educational indicators. For example, the who, what, and where of existing STC-related efforts in the area were broadly enumerated as to number of stakeholders involved, the number and rate of activities, and the amount of economic resources available. Other analyses revealed prevalence rates of high school completion, college entrance, college completion, youth unemployment, entry-level openings, and other indicators of strengths and weaknesses of the local ecology. All in all, the needs assessment dug up data for and gave direction to the articulation of policy.

Articulation of Policy

Policy has been defined as "prudence or wisdom in the management of affairs; a definite course or method of action selected from among alternatives and in light of given conditions to guide and determine present and future decisions" (*Merriam Webster's Collegiate Dictionary*, 1996). In constructing an intervention, this is the building code stage: the identification and delineation of optimal structural and functional arrangements. The articulation of policy is aided by a standardized and systematic code. Our search of the intervention planning and evaluation literature failed to find a consistent, user-friendly code. Therefore, we operationalized a set of terms

as a template for planners to describe their intervention. These terms included mission statement, core values and guiding principles, organizational and intervention specifications, goals, objectives, activities, outcomes, and benchmarks. In addition to the following definitions and descriptions, STC examples of these terms are given in Table 1.

A *mission statement* is a broad, yet focused, statement of purpose, a reason for being. The Partnership's mission is to: "Foster and guide a metropolitan-wide system to better link businesses, schools and the community

TABLE 1

Sample Policy Template for Building an Intervention within the Context of School-To-Career

Mission statement.
Foster and guide a metropolitan-wide system to better link businesses, schools and the community so that our young people and our region are better equipped to prosper in a global economy.

Core value and guiding principle.
Learning occurs when it is contextual and connected–relevancy is key.

Organizational stewarding and intervention description.
A multi-model, stakeholder-driven, collaborative process of academic and experiential learning is connected by activities at and new regularities between individual, organizational, and systemic domains.

Systemic goal.
The Partnership will facilitate change in the culture of and resource allocation for educational delivery around STC core values and guiding principles.
Objective. Increase capacity to organize educational delivery around contextualized experiences.
Activity. Provide structured educator externship opportunities.
Process outcome. 100 educators participate in a 2-week, full-time work experience.
Effect outcome. An employer–educator collaborative curriculum is developed.

Organizational goal.
"Classroom" becomes an array of community venues.
Objective. Students will be exposed to a variety of active learning environments.
Activity. Students experience a work-site job shadow.
Process outcome. 1000 students participate in a daylong job shadow.
Effect outcome. Students define classroom and learning in non-traditional ways.

Individual goal.
Students are better prepared for post-secondary success.
Objective. Students amass theoretical and experiential skills that qualify them for a range of post-secondary options.
Activity. An educator externship results in a relevant, contextualized problem-based learning project for students.
Process outcome. 10,000 students experience 10 critical learning projects each semester.
Effect outcome. Students improve academic and performance scores.

so that our young people and our region are better equipped to prosper in a global economy" (BE²:STCP, 1998b, p. 1).

Core values and guiding principles are the premises that permeate and govern the organizational and intervention infrastructure. Often these operate beyond conscious consideration, yet they can be critical elements in dissemination fidelity (e.g., Bauman, Stein, & Ireys, 1991). The core values and principles of The Partnership are premised on pedagogical, collaboration, and systems change evidence, for example, that learning is not just a classroom phenomenon; it needs to be woven within a community network of experiences.

Organizational and intervention specifications describe the structures or functions of the stewarding organization(s) and the intervention itself. Organizational and intervention specifications establish quality control standards and define the operational domain just as construction specifications establish building material standards and, for example, whether penthouse windows are to be fixed-framed or operable. An intervention specification example is given in Table 1. A stewarding specification can take the form of an organizational chart or exposition, such as

The Partnership is a 501(c)(3) organization with a policy and fundraising board (i.e., Board of Directors), an administrative committee (i.e., the Metropolitan Management Team), a coalition of local partnerships (e.g., school districts and other partners, in consortia or as individual entities), and Partner Organizations (e.g., parents, youth, labor, civic, philanthropic), and an implementational body comprised of nine functional teams.

Goals are the ends toward which efforts are directed and toward which there may be multiple paths. Typically, goals are indirectly measured or inferred from having met one or an aggregation of any number of relevant objectives. For example, the goal of optimizing post secondary success may be measured by the acquisition of one or more specific skills. Representative goals of The Partnership relative to individual, organizational, and system domains are given in Table 1.

Objectives are strategic positions or purposes sought in the pursuit of a goal. *General objectives* are tangible and directly, yet flexibly, assessable phenomenon from which specific measures and outcomes may be derived. *Specific objectives* are contextually determined manifestations of a specific activity. General objectives may be achievable through any one or more relevant activities and by virtue of accomplishing any one or more specific objectives. For example, balancing a financial account (*specific objective*) or calculating a project cost (*specific objective*) may achieve, jointly or severally, the objective of applying mathematical procedures (*general objective*).

Activities are acts designed to achieve an objective or maintain the organizational or intervention infrastructure. Like objectives, activities can be general or specific. For example, a student summer internship (*general activity*) may require the student to staff the switchboard (*specific activity*) for the purpose of applying conversational skills (*specific objective*) as partial satisfaction of the application of a repertoire of communication skills (*general objective*), which serves the goal of making contextual connection and gaining appreciation for a curriculum of discourse analysis (*goal*). It is essential, even if tedious, to operationalize activities. For example, what constitutes having had a structured workplace learning experience? Does a 1-hr site visit in which an educator tours a facility constitute such an activity, or does it require a summer-long internship of hands-on learning and formal instruction?

Outcomes are data that document the nature and extent of a process or effect. Outcomes derive from and reflect back on objectives. *Process outcomes* emerge from the pursuit of objectives—that is, from activities—as these relate to the targets of intervention. For example, intervention intensity might be assessed as the number of different activities participated in (*nature*) and the duration of that participation (*extent*). *Effect outcomes* emerge from the targets of intervention as these relate to change on some variable of interest, or as they manifest as a product. Targets can be individuals, organizations, the system-at-large, or their governing regularities (Seidman, 1988). For example, students may show an increase in educational enthusiasm, standardized test scores, or employability. Organizationally, the operation of the "classroom" may have expanded beyond the traditional hallowed halls. Systemically, state academic standards may have become modeled on authentic learning and assessment methodology (e.g., Gordon, 1998; Newmann & Wehlage, 1993), such as problem- or project-based learning (e.g., Blumenfeld et al., 1991; Fogarty, 1997), critical thinking (Sternberg & Spear-Swerling, 1996), and portfolio or public exhibit assessment (Paris & Ayres, 1994).

Benchmarks are established criteria for determining that a goal or objective has been met or an outcome was consequential. One objective of The Partnership is to engage educators in the metropolitan Kansas City area in structured workplace learning experiences. If one educator, or two or three, were so engaged, would the objective have been achieved? Answers to benchmark questions such as this are relative, hinge on a multitude of factors, and must be realistically established *a priori*. The Partnership has established a benchmark of 3,000, or 15%, area educators so engaged by the year 2001.

In addition, it needs to be determined whether an outcome was consequential. For example, effects on educators who have engaged in a structured workplace experience might be an alteration in their lesson plans
(*behavioral*) or increased enthusiasm to incorporate a contextual component in their lesson plans (*attitudinal*) or an increase in the relevant knowledge of a subject matter (*cognitional*). Each of these effect outcomes can be,
and traditionally have been, assessed by standard statistical significance
benchmarks (e.g., $p < .05$ for chi-square, t test, and other procedures as appropriate), although in some cases alternative benchmark processes and
parameters, such as effect size, may be of value.

Our building code of terminology can be easily converted to any intervention context, thus rendering a clear and comprehensive blueprint for
action. It is especially critical to note that the general and specific distinc-
tion for objectives and activities is not trivial. It is the general that, for example, allows for a curricula, and the specific that allows for an
independent plan of study. It is the general that provides a standard pedagogy and the specific that permits presentational autonomy. It is the general that supplies the intervention its strength, the specific its flexibility.

IMPLEMENTING

The Partnership Initiative uses an ecological implementation approach
across three general domains or strata: individual, organizational, and system. As an ecology, these strata are not independent. Neither is one the ag-
gregate manifestation of another. For example, the assemblage of 100 individuals does not constitute an organization. Similarly, although
constituting a different philosophical argument, one is not reducible to another—that is, a system cannot be completely explained in terms of organizations or individuals. That is, we cannot rely simply on a trickle-down effect in which organizational and individual change results from system
intercession, nor can we rely on a critical mass effect in which organizational and system change results from individual intercession.

A guiding principle of The Partnership's initiative is that an intervention that is constructed holistically, as a coordinated model of direct and
indirect effects through intercession at multiple strata simultaneously, will
be more efficacious and enduring.

An understanding of, and strategy for, ecological change can be guided
by an appropriate heuristic, for example, Rogers' (1995) diffusion theory,
Seidman's (1987) locus of intervention and effect model, or Thagard's
(1992) theory of conceptual change. We introduce a heuristic based on assimilation and accommodation. The *"assimmodation"* heuristic is in a pre-

liminary stage of development. When applied to planning, implementing, and evaluating an intervention, we believe it has intrinsic value and utility. Plans to gather empirical support are being prepared by Charles T. Diebold, who originated the heuristic and its resultant model.

Assimmodation: A Model of Ecological Innovation and Change

Fundamentally, PIE is a process of assimilation and accommodation. For our purposes, assimilation is the fitting of new information or processes to existing structure (i.e., containment), whereas accommodation is the adjustment of structure to fit new information or process (i.e., change). Structure can be a cognitive schema, an organizational flow chart, pedagogy, curricula, roles, systemic regularities, and so on. In our construction analogy, assimilation is redecorating or rearranging the furniture, whereas ac-

TABLE 2
Assimmodation Innovation Model (AIM)

Accommodation Altitude	Assimilation Latitude	
	Low	High
Low	**Type I** Inconsequential *variation* Tradition Maintenance Status quo Platonic Form Immutable Universalistic	**Type II** Quantitative variation Summative Linear, Continuous Exclusive Specialization Putting eggs in one basket Molecular Reductionistic
High	**Type III** Qualitative change Novelty Quantum leap Discontinuity Impulsivity Midlife crisis Revolution Idiographic Anarchistic	**Type IV** Integrative change Ecological Multi-disciplinary Diversification Inclusive Evolution Empowering Emergent

commodation is removing a partition wall or adding a wing. *Assimmodation* is both, that is, rearranging the furniture within a newly expanded space.

Table 2 presents the assimmodation innovation model (AIM); a 2×2 matrix that typecasts four innovation and change thresholds across interrelations of high and low levels of assimilation and accommodation. Type I and Type II correspond to containment, whereas Type III and Type IV represent change. To further distinguish the AIM types, the table provides a list of descriptive characteristics.

Type I is inconsequential variation and is characterized by descriptors such as strict adherence to tradition; maintenance of the status quo; Platonism; and/or by immutable, universalistic philosophies. At an individual stratum, this may manifest as strictly genetic or trait descriptions or explanations of educational capacity. Organizationally, it might reify classroom or school, that is, regard them as specific physical entities. Systemically, it might preclude community collaboration in curriculum development by relegating such solely to the purview of individual teachers.

Type II is quantitative variation and is characterized by descriptors such as summative; linear; continuous; exclusive; specialization; putting all your eggs in one basket; and/or by strictly molecular, reductionist philosophies. In education, "earlier efforts that sought to extend the benefits of the current system to excluded groups or that worked to increase the quantity of education received by all children" (Shields, 1994, p. 1) were Type II reforms.

Type III is qualitative change and is characteristic of novelty; quantum leap; discontinuity; impulsivity; midlife crisis; revolution; and/or by idiographic, anarchist philosophies. Just as is the case for Type I and Type II, Type III characteristics can be perceived as positive or negative. In certain contexts or situations, one type may be more appropriate than another. Type IV capitalizes on combined advantage.

By its very nature, Type IV represents a perpetual process for innovation and change that is rooted in, and emerges from, the context and history of Types I–III. Type IV is integrative change and is characterized by descriptors such as ecological; multidisciplinary; diversified; inclusive; evolutionary; and/or by empowering, emergent philosophies. Community psychology, economic globalization, and The Partnership's Initiative are examples of Type IV. For sustained systematic development, Type IV is ideal when planning, implementing, and evaluating an intervention.

Moreover, assessing the ecological capacity for change, that is, the assimmodation innovation capacity (AIC), is a critical consideration in the PIE process. If Type I is the prevalent AIC, there may be limits to what can be successfully planned, implemented, and evaluated. For example, attempting to assimilate community-based learning opportunities into the educational repertoire of educators and students will be unsuccessful if accommodations in classroom boundaries, pedagogical practice, class schedule routines, and offsite transportation are not made. Similarly, it would be inappropriate to expect students to define the classroom in nontraditional ways (*effect outcome*) if classroom AIC allowed only for the traditional conceptualization.

AIC can be quantitatively and qualitatively assessed by using common content analysis procedures of an intervention's policy template (i.e., mission, goals, objectives, activities, benchmarks, outcomes, etc.).

The AIM model of change as *type* is distinct from models of change as stage, or as being hierarchical, summative, or linear in nature (cf. Prochaska, DiClemente, & Norcross, 1992; Rogers, 1995). Moreover, despite the conundrum that AIM assimilates prediction and explanation of change within its own structural matrix, assimilation and accommodation capacities (i.e., ecological AIC) clearly affect initiation, diffusion, and maintenance of an intervention and need to be taken into account when constructing the organizational and intervention infrastructures.

Constructing the Organizational Stewarding Infrastructure

The organizational stewarding infrastructure must be built to support the core values and the guiding principles of the Initiative. The stewards are the stakeholders, the system of reinforced concrete piers cast clear to bedrock that a skyscraper rests upon. Obviously, one pier or one stakeholder—like a single stack of blocks—limits the type of building or intervention that can be constructed. The Partnership wanted an assemblage of stakeholders that would create collaborative advantage for the construction of a vast ecological infrastructure.

Stakeholder assemblage. In intervention planning, the identification of stakeholders at an early stage is critical to ensure a complete understanding of the intervention definition and process (Finn, 1996). Paradoxically, the intervention is often not defined well enough at coalition commencement "to ensure that all necessary actors are actually 'at the table'" (Finn, 1996, p. 154). It is the ongoing task of the catalyst organization, or "policy entrepreneur" [to use Sink's (1991) term], to energize and build an ecologically valid coalition. In our construction analogy, this is akin to a general contractor assembling appropriate subcontractors.

As an aid to stakeholder assemblage, Finn (1996) has detailed a two-step process of stakeholder (a) identification and (b) influence mapping, and Himmelman (1996) has prescribed 20 steps in designing a collaborative. In the fall of 1995, The Partnership relied on its earlier needs assessment and snowball techniques to assemble stakeholders. For example, the catalog of STC-related activity compiled for the metro area, along with focus group input, resulted in over 50 groups and organizations becoming actively involved in The Partnership's initial efforts. These stakeholders included students; parents; classroom educators; representatives from educational agencies and institutions; employers; employer organizations (e.g.; Chamber of Commerce); labor representatives; community organizations and councils (e.g.; Kansas City Regional Professional Development Center; Mid-America Regional Council); foundations; federal, state and local government agencies; and youth organizations and centers (e.g., YouthNet, YMCA YouthFriends).

Furthermore, The Partnership detailed a list of roles and responsibilities for each stakeholder group. For example, parents and students were expected to serve on site-based councils and to participate in operating and governance bodies; the Full Employment Council was expected to be a business sector advocate and to participate in the development of school curricula; metropolitan colleges and universities were expected to execute articulation agreements and to provide new professional development opportunities; YMCA YouthFriends was expected to recruit, train, and match volunteer mentors with students; and The Learning Exchange was expected to provide leadership, technical assistance, and collaborative management.

The articulation of roles and responsibilities is a key factor in coalition development (Butterfoss, Goodman, & Wandersman, 1993). It is not enough to simply elicit initial input from stakeholders. The Partnership sought to ensure continuous stakeholder involvement through an administrative structure intended to create and maintain collaborative advantage.

Collaborative advantage. "Collaborative advantage is concerned with the creation of synergy between collaborating organizations" (Huxham, 1996, p. 14). Himmelman (1996) specifically differentiated a continuum of synergy from networking, to coordination, to cooperation, and finally to collaboration. He defined collaboration as "exchanging information, altering activities, sharing resources, and enhancing the capacity of another for mutual benefit and to achieve a common purpose" (p. 28).

Additionally, the term *partnership* implies joint commitment, owner-ship, and accountability. The Partnership created collaborative advantage principally through the creation of functional teams.

Functional teams.   The functional team framework is the infrastructure through which committed community stakeholders and Partnership staff plan, implement, and evaluate the Initiative. Basically, the framework consists of a set of nine functional teams that divide among themselves critical components of work, tapping individual strengths and competencies, so that The Partnership can simultaneously address a variety of agendas. The nine teams include (a) all student inclusion; (b) benchmarks and evaluations; (c) employer and partner linkages; (d) marketing and communications; (e) postsecondary linkages; (f) professional development, design, and support; (g) resource development; (h) school-based instruction, content standards, and assessment practices; and (i) work-based learning, design and support. Individualized charters guide each functional team (see Table 3).

Functional teams are staffed by an STC consultant from The Learning Exchange or local partner (constituting the day-to-day production and administrative arm of The Partnership); however, each is chaired by a volunteer community member. On average, teams consist of 7 to 12 members, representing a variety of stakeholder groups, and formally meet once a month, yet often are in contact weekly or even daily. The focus of each team is typically on fostering organizational or system strata infusion of STC principles and activities and to provide technical support and collaborative network linkage. Some of the members hold full-time positions with their respective organizations as STC coordinator or liaison and oversee the implementation of specific components of the Initiative (e.g., mentoring, project-based classroom curricula).

The Functional team approach provides Type IV AIC advantages by assimilating the ordinary duties and responsibilities of stakeholders into accommodative, collaborative structures and directed function. Further bolstering the capacity for Type IV innovation and change is the assimmodation of functional teams, metropolitan management teams, and boards of directors into one another's separate charters and operations. A representative from the board of directors, the chair and staff member of each functional team, and representatives from formal local partnerships (e.g., school district or other organizations who received federal or state STC grants) comprise the metropolitan management team, which serves as an administrative committee principally charged with creating and sus-

TABLE 3
Functional Team Charters

All student inclusion functional team:
Identify and provide support and expertise to the other functional teams to ensure successful participation for all students.

Benchmarks and evaluations functional team:
Develop both a regional evaluation plan with benchmarks and a model(s) for local partnerships and school districts.

Employer and partner linkages functional team:
Seek out an ever-widening circle of employers and other partners (union, community-based organizations, professional organizations, entrepreneurs, and families) who can be involved at many levels in providing activities that connect students, educators, and employers to support both education and workforce development.

Marketing and communications functional team:
Develop a marketing plan with materials and clear messages about the school-to-career initiative that persuade key stakeholders to measurably change school-to-career behaviors.

Postsecondary linkages functional team:
Audit existing articulation agreements and support new agreements that provide seamless pathways for students, address the issue of postsecondary institutions' admission requirements that inhibit STC, and promote preservice teacher professional development experiences that connect learning with earning.

Professional development, design, and support functional team:
Develop a framework of professional development experiences that expose educators to a variety of workplaces, support their use of new instructional practices for applied as well as traditional academic learning, and facilitate career counseling of students with the ultimate goal of more career options.

Resource development functional team:
Bring together private, federal, and state funders with school systems and workforce development and training agencies to reallocate, defragment, and develop new resource strategies for the school-to-career initiative.

School-based instruction, content standards, and assessment practices functional team:
Look for long-term approaches for developing curricula, instructional practices, and assessments that meet world-class standards while providing students with a sense of relevance.

Work-based learning, design and support functional team:
Develop, identify, and/or coordinate learning opportunities for students in a work environment that is integrated with, and adds value to, school-site instruction and assessment practices.

taining collaborative advantage among its constituent members. This second-order coalition of stakeholders informs the board of directors (a third-order coalition) of the direction and needs of the Initiative. In turn, the board is charged with promoting the vision, paving the political way, and leveraging funds.

A sound stewarding infrastructure is a necessary, even if insufficient, condition for a sound intervention infrastructure.

Constructing the Intervention Infrastructure

STC is a broad array of pedagogical, curricular, and learning strategies and activities. It is not a prepackaged program of products and services. To implement it as such would be remiss and miss the mark. The functional team charters begin to convey the scope of STC components and activities. Implementing an array of educational strategies (i.e., a system) into an existing educational system is a challenge. The Partnership took advantage of the existing system's AIC potentials.

For example, at the system stratum, The Partnership implemented STC compatibly with the legislated goals and the objectives of the departments of education in Kansas and Missouri. Specifically, The Partnership has been able to point out how the Initiative's emphasis on key requirements of Missouri's A+ Schools Program—that is, career development, relevancy, specification of knowledge, skills and competencies, measurable performance standards, and community partnership—can help schools and districts achieve A+ status and the accompanying grant awards. More specifically, The Partnership has capitalized on compatibility with state-specified performance and knowledge standards. For example, Missouri organized 35 objectives under four performance goals:

1. Gather, analyze, and apply information and ideas.
2. Communicate effectively within and beyond the classroom.
3. Recognize and solve problems.
4. Make decisions and act as responsible members of society.

Organizationally, perhaps the single greatest accommodation challenge of the Initiative has been, and remains, collaboration. How do you get teachers, psychologists, politicians, business persons, and other community stakeholders to collaborate in educational reform? First and foremost, The Partnership determined that, to implement collaboration, it must itself collaborate. This entails a peculiar challenge. Administering a collaborative effort involves a different set of administrative skills than the ones traditionally acquired as well as collaborative skills themselves. Moreover, even while trying to master this peculiar juggling act of administering and collaborating simultaneously, The Partnership staff (e.g., The Learning Exchange) has had to provide technical assistance in STC pedagogy and curricula, including collaboration, to other Partnership members.

Technical assistance in accommodative curricula development is a collaborative case in point, actually two points. First, when an Initiative partner (e.g., a classroom educator) requests curricula assistance he or she often has assimilation, rather than accommodation, in mind. That is, he or she may be expecting "a solution," such as an activity or a workbook, that "fits". Rather than fitting partners with products, The Partnership engages partners in a process of curricula design that parallels the overarching planning, implementing, and evaluating processes described herein (e.g., needs assessment; stakeholder articulation of goals, objectives, activities, and outcomes; constructing the stewarding and intervening infrastructures; calibrating and correcting through evaluation). Our overarching PIE infrastructure, and the AIC model, are as applicable to building an ecological intervention as they are to building one educator's lesson plan.

Second, a most effective augmentation of the process of curricula design is collaboratively facilitating a personalized, experiential opportunity from which a relevant curriculum develops. For example, 74 "externships" during the summer of 1998 connected classroom educators with an extended community opportunity to practice what they teach, and then teach what they practiced.

The educators were integrally involved in designing the extern experience, in collaboration with a business or community organization. Donning a critical learning role, as contrasted with traditional learning roles (Table 4), represents an STC pedagogical practice in that it emphasizes a learned rather than taught experience. Assimmodating the method into the educators' own professional development appeared to have had parallel assimmodative transfer into the lesson plans they developed for students (BE^2:STCP, 1998a).

For example, an extern at a chemical testing laboratory found a new excitement and envisioned multiple ways with which to integrate her experience into her high school chemistry and science curriculum. Particularly, she was impressed with the chemical complexities of a substance that we take for granted, water. In testing for water purity, she had been reminded of the methodological rigor and scientific precision required for valid conclusions. Rather than asking "Did I *get* it right?" she intends her students to ask "Did I *do* it right?" Similar attention and rigor is emphasized in intervention evaluation.

164   DIEBOLD ET AL.

TABLE 4
Teacher/Student Roles in Traditional Versus Critical Learning Methods

Traditional Learning	Critical Learning
Teacher knows answer.	No one knows the answer.
Students routinely work in isolation.	Students routinely work with others, including teachers, peers, and community members.
Teacher plans all activities and projects.	Students and teacher plan and negotiate activities and projects.
Teacher decides method of assessment.	Students routinely assess themselves and negotiate summative evaluations.
Information is organized, interpreted, and communicated by teacher to students.	Information is acquired, organized, interpreted, and communicated by students to appropriate audience(s).
Reading, writing, and mathematics are treated as separate disciplines; listening and speaking as separate processes.	Integrated merging of all disciplines is necessary for problem solving; listening and speaking are tandem to learning.
Thinking is usually theoretical and syllogistic.	Thinking involves problem solving, reasoning, and decision making.

Note. From *The Employer's Role in Linking School and Work: A Policy Statement by the Research and Policy Committee of the Committee for Economic Development* (p.19). By Committee for Economic Development, 1998, New York: Author. Copyright 1998 by the Committee for Economic Development. Adapted with permission.

EVALUATING

"Evaluation is a fundamental part of curriculum development, not an appendage" (Cronbach, 1963, p. 683). So, too, is evaluation a fundamental part of an intervention. The Partnership has diffused evaluation throughout its components, including the 6-week coordinated, work-based and school-based enrichment for students and the summer educator "externships" cited previously. Data are constantly collected and used for decision making. In addition, a comprehensive, multi-year, external evaluation of The Partnership Initiative is underway.

Whether explicit or implicit, all evaluation theories and methods impose a "logic model," or floor plan. A logic model specifically derives from the mission, goals, objectives, activities, and desired outcomes articulated in the intervention building code. A *logic model* specifies the theoretical, empirical, and operational linkages of units within an ecological infrastructure that are used to predict, explain, or infer the consequentiality of process and effect outcomes. Where evaluation theories and methods differ is in operationalizing and documenting "consequentiality." Consequentiality established a priori in the form of benchmarks and documentation that is systematic, robust, and thorough will minimize a posteriori conclusions conflict. Conflict is also reduced by appropriately calibrating the evaluation to stakeholder purpose, intervention logic model, and AIC potential.

Calibration

If stakeholders are engaged in planning, implementing, and evaluating, then subsequent data are likely to be authentic. Stakeholders include evaluators, whether internal or external to the initiative. In fact, if evaluators are assembled into the PIE process as soon as possible after conception, a more ecologically balanced intervention is likely to result. The benchmarks and evaluations functional team has served that role in The Partnership's Initiative and has been a major influence on the establishment and assessment of the agenda of other functional teams.

Although we recommend stakeholder selection of a particular philosophy of evaluation—for example, experiment based (Fairweather & Davidson, 1986), realist based (Pawson & Tilley, 1997), use based (Patton, 1997), empowerment based (Fetterman, Kaftarian, & Wandersman, 1996), or the evaluation philosophies of Scriven, Campbell, Weiss, Wholey, Stake, Cronbach, or Rossi (each reviewed in Shadish, Cook, & Leviton, 1995)—we do so with the caveat that the selection be "an evaluation," not a poll or a descriptive, historical chronicle. Evaluation is distinguished from the latter types by virtue of having a logic model. This rightly implies that an evaluation must be logically designed and methodically detailed. Design and method are often confused.

Designs include case study, pretest–posttest, comparison groups, time series, and the like (e.g., Cook & Campbell, 1979; Isaac & Michael, 1995). Methods include direct observation; interviewing; surveying; experiencing; and content-, archival-, and meta-analysis (e.g., Creswell, 1998; Denzin & Lincoln, 1994). Together, design and method impart confidence in logic model conclusions (i.e., prediction, explanation, inference). No design or method is without limitation; compatibility of design and method is paramount, and relevance to the articulated policy and the logic model is essential. Ideally, one should strive for an ecology of purpose, design, and method. The Partnership has incorporated most of these designs and methods into one component or another of the Initiative.

One example was a pretest–posttest survey of an integrated work-based and school-based, 6-week summer internship for middle and high school students. To ensure relevance to AIC potential, survey questions were selected based on their responsiveness to general STC principles and practices and to stated objectives and expected outcomes of the program, especially as reflected in activity and curriculum outlines. Both process and effect outcomes were represented in the survey. For example, process components included work site and school attendance (*extent*), and work site and school activities (*nature*). Effect components included (a) cognitional items concerning general relationships between school and work (e.g., relatedness of rules at school and rules at work), specific connections (e.g., ways in which math is used at work), and contextual awareness (e.g., the importance of deadlines and schedules); (b) attitudinal items, such as attitudes toward the process and effect of cooperation; (c) behavioral items concerning personal behavior (e.g., likelihood of motivating, teasing, teaching, or fighting with others) and skill development (e.g., being a leader, solving a real-world problem, specifying steps to reach a goal); and (d) theoretical construct items that tapped a sense of community. In general, outcomes were not assessed by single items, but by composites of related items. Furthermore, for triangulation purposes, somewhat parallel surveys were administered to employer and educator participants.

The results were not used to find fault, but to inform corrections, that is, to rearrange (assimilate) or remodel (accommodate) the intervention's floor plan.

Correction

Evaluation purpose, design, or details can be modified. In turn, these will affect intervention activities and objectives and perhaps even goals; organizational stewarding; and intervention specifications, mission, and logic model.

For example, findings from the aforementioned summer program resulted in recommended corrections to design, details, certain objectives, certain activities, and more deliberate logic model linkages. The pretest–posttest design was most severely limited in its sole reliance on self-report. Validity of interpretations would have been enhanced if there had been concurrent field observations. Students, teachers, and employers did not always share the same objectives. To be fair, many did embrace common objectives, but disparity was evident in some students just wanting to earn a bit of money, teachers wanting to make real connections between school and work, and some employers just wanting cheap peak summer help. There is nothing necessarily wrong with any of these objectives, and if properly taken into account and deliberately and collaboratively woven into the intervention, everyone can help achieve one another's agendas. The latter entails a change in certain activities. For example, more planning, especially the disclosure of expectations was recommended. More specifically, the school-based and the work-based activities were not explicitly coordinated to ensure that "connections" would be made, for example, how math or science is used at work, resulting in a recommendation that the logic model, or floor plan, be more precise.

IMPLICATIONS

In titling this article Building an *Intervention…* we assimilated the conventional vernacular. We would prefer our title to read Building an *Innovation…*, which is the image we most want to leave with you. Semantics make an AIC difference. Rappaport (1985) explicated such, relative to the power of empowerment language; Diebold (1998a) relative to the term *health promotion* over *prevention;* and Elias (1997) relative to terminology, such as intervention, diffusion, dissemination, and the like. *Innovation* implies "renewal," whereas *intervention* implies a "coming between," and, to the extent the latter is perceived to be one's intent, it is likely to be resisted by others (Elias, 1997). We seek to build innovation.

To build an innovation, one must discern the local ecology's AIC. In construction, the load capacity of the foundational bedrock determines whether 1 or 100 floors can be constructed; in social interventions, ecological AIC determines whether a Type I, II, III, or IV innovation is constructible. For example, how one defines an issue also defines one's AIC. If poor student achievement is defined as insufficient teaching time, then AIC will only support the likes of Type I, status quo of "teaching" (as different from, for example, educating, mentoring, etc.) and the Type II lengthening of the school day and/or year. Similarly, defining an innovation tends to define the issue, even if implicitly. For example, merely distributing a list of career opportunities suggests that the educational status quo is fine and that students simply need a directory of names and addresses for the successful transition from school to career.

Defining issues and innovations is not as simple as just exemplified. Our infrastructure of planning, implementing, and evaluating provides a theoretical and practical blueprint for dialectically defining and refining issues and innovations. Table 5 is a checklist of the construction process, albeit linearly and devoid of intended ecological dynamics. If these key elements were superimposed on an architectural rendering, there would be no penthouse. Constructing an ecologically valid innovation pre-

TABLE 5

Building an Intervention: A Blueprint for Planning, Implementing, and Evaluating

Planning.
 Theoretical and empirical grounding.
  Ground issue or condition in relevant theory(ies).
  Ground issue or condition in empirical best practices.
 Needs assessment.
  Identify parallel efforts within the local ecology.
  Identify all stakeholders in the local ecology.
  Determine nature and extent of need.
   Identify human, material & fiscal resources.
   Examine social indicators.
   Determine stakeholder expectations.
   Determine intervention barriers.
 Articulate policy.
  Mission statement.
  Core values and guiding principles.
  Organizational stewarding and intervention specifications.
  Goals.
  Objectives (general and specific).
  Outcomes (process and effect).
  Activities (general and specific).
  Benchmarks.
Implementing.
 Construct the stewarding infrastructure.
  Assemble stakeholders.
  Specify roles and responsibilities.
  Organize for collaborative advantage.
 Construct the intervention infrastructure.
  Delineate assimmodation innovation capacities.
  Intercede at multiple strata simultaneously.
Evaluating.
 Establish logic model.
 Select an evaluation purpose, design, and methodology.
 Calibrate evaluation instruments and procedures.
 Analyze evaluation data for desired and unanticipated effects.
 Correct intervention as needed.
Re-plan, Re-implement, Re-evaluate.

cludes ever topping out. A Type IV AIC is a dynamic, self-perpetuating force.

The Partnership's Initiative is an ecology of multiples: (a) multiple stakeholders (e.g., students, parents, educators, business people), (b) multiple disciplines (e.g., education, psychology, economics), (c) multiple values, (d) multiple goals and objectives, (e) multiple activities, (f) multiple theoretical and empirical foundations, (g) multiple venues (e.g., school, workplace, community), (h) multiple outcomes, (i) multiple loci of intervention and effect (e.g., individual, organizational, system, connecting regularities), and (j) multiple stewards. Each of these preclude dichotomous propensities, for example, top-down versus bottom-up, in favor of dialectic realities.

In similar dialectic fashion, let us expand the intellectual universe of those whose education is entrusted to our stewardship and in so doing empower them to construct a rewarding and full life of their own design and choice.

ACKNOWLEDGMENTS

The statements contained in this report do not necessarily reflect the views of the Board of Directors of the Business/Education Expectations (BE[2]): School-To-Career Partnership, the Board of Directors of The Learning Exchange, or the regents of the University of Missouri- Kansas City. This report was supported in part by a University of Missouri-Kansas City & The Learning Exchange Studies in Community Change Fellowship, and by a U. S. Departments of Labor & Education Urban/Rural Opportunities Grant (84-278D). We thank The Partnership's School-To-Career staff upon whose work and input this report rests: Mary Blomquist, Bev Clevenger, Rose Joanning, Carol Lovett, Stephanie Mallory, Brook Moody, Joyce Richmond, Becky Schimmel, Virginia Slind, Glenda Vinson, and David Washington of The Learning Exchange; Ricki Dreyfus and Alicia Melgoza of the Full Employment Council; Tawanna Strode of Junior Achievement; Walt Tabory of YMCA YouthFriends; and all other contributors to the Kansas City Metropolitan Region School-To-Career Initiative.

REFERENCES

Bauman, L. J., Stein, R. E. K., & Ireys, H. T. (1991). Reinventing fidelity: The transfer of social technology among settings. *American Journal of Community Psychology, 19*, 619–639.

BE[2]:School-To-Career Partnership of Kansas City. (1996, January). *U. S. Departments of Labor & Education comprehensive school-to-work urban/rural opportunities grant application.* Kansas City, MO: The Learning Exchange.

BE[2]:School-To-Career Partnership. (1998a, Summer). *Educator externships, educator products: Classroom topics, projects, and lesson plans.* Kansas City, MO: The Learning Exchange.

BE^2:School-To-Career Partnership. (1998b, October). *Vision and mission*. Kansas City, MO: The Learning Exchange.

BE^2:School-To-Career Partnership. (1998c). What is school-to-career? *The Motivator*, 2(2), 6.

Blumenfeld, P. C., Soloway, E., Marx, R. W., Krajcik, J. S., Guzdial, M., & Palincsar, A. (1991). Motivating project based learning: Sustaining the doing, supporting the learning. *Educational Psychologist*, 25, 369–398.

Butterfoss, F. D., Goodman, R. M., & Wandersman, A. (1993). Community coalitions for prevention and health promotion. *Health Education Research: Theory and Practice, 8*, 315– 330.

Cook, T. D., & Campbell, D. T. (1979). *Quasi-experimentation: Design & analysis issues for field settings*. Boston: Houghton Mifflin.

Creswell, J. W. (1998). *Qualitative inquiry and research design: Choosing among five traditions*. Thousand Oaks, CA: Sage.

Cronbach, L. J. (1963). Course improvement through evaluation. *Teachers College Record, 64*, 672–683.

Denzin, N. K., & Lincoln, Y. S. (Eds.). (1994). *Handbook of qualitative research*. Thousand Oaks, CA: Sage.

Diebold, C. T. (1998a). Health promotion over prevention, standing up for empowering semantics and operations: Comment on Cowen. *The Community Psychologist, 31*, 6–9.

Diebold, C. T. (1998b). *Jobs to career 1998 summer instructional support program: Evaluation report*. Kansas City, MO: The Learning Exchange.

Elias, M. (1997). Reinterpreting dissemination of prevention programs as widespread implementation with effectiveness and fidelity. In R. P. Weissberg, T. P. Gullotta, R. L. Hampton, B. A. Ryan, & G. R. Adams (Eds), *Establishing preventive services* (pp. 253–289). Thousand Oaks, CA: Sage.

Fairweather, G. W., & Davidson, W. (1986). *Community experimentation: Theory, methods, and practice*. New York: McGraw-Hill.

Fetterman, D. M., Kaftarian, S. J., & Wandersman, A. (Eds.). (1996). *Empowerment evaluation: Knowledge and tools for self-assessment & accountability*. Thousand Oaks, CA: Sage.

Finn, C. B. (1996). Utilizing stakeholder strategies for positive collaborative outcomes. In C. Huxham (Ed.), *Creating collaborative advantage* (pp. 152–164). Thousand Oaks, CA: Sage.

Fogarty, R. (1997). *Problem-based learning and other curriculum models for the multiple intelligences classroom*. Arlington Heights, IL: IRI/Skylight Training and Publishing.

Gordon, R. (1998). Balancing real-world problems with real-world results. *Phi Delta Kappan, 79*, 390–393.

Himmelman, A. T. (1996). On the theory and practice of transformational collaboration: From social service to social justice. In C. Huxham (Ed.), *Creating collaborative advantage* (pp. 19–43). Thousand Oaks, CA: Sage.

Huxham, C. (1996). Collaboration and collaborative advantage. In C. Huxham (Ed.), *Creating collaborative advantage* (pp. 1–18). Thousand Oaks, CA: Sage.

Isaac, S., & Michael, W. B. (1995). *Handbook in research and evaluation* (3rd ed.). San Diego, CA: Educational and Industrial Testing Services.

Kansas City Regional School-To-Career Partnership. (1995, June). *Final report and plan: Kansas City regional school-to-career partnership*. Kansas City, MO: Author.

Merriam Webster's collegiate dictionary (10th ed.). (1996). Springfield, MA: Merriam

Newmann, F. M., & Wehlage, G. G. (1993). Five standards of authentic instruction. *Educational Leadership, 50*(7), 8–12.

Paris, S. G., & Ayres, L. R. (1994). *Becoming reflective students and teachers with portfolios and authentic assessment*. Washington, DC: American Psychological Association.

Patton, M. Q. (1997). *Utilization-focused evaluation: The new century text* (3rd ed.). Thousand Oaks, CA: Sage.

Pawson, R., & Tilley, N. (1997). *Realistic evaluation.* Thousand Oaks, CA: Sage.

Price, R. H. (1987). Linking intervention research and risk factor research. In J. A. Steinberg & M. M. Silverman (Eds.), *Preventing mental disorder. A research perspective* (DHHS Publication No. ADM 87-1492, pp. 48–56). Washington, DC: U.S. Government Printing Office.

Prochaska, J. O., DiClemente, C. C., & Norcross, J. C. (1992). In search of how people change: Applications to addictive behaviors. *American Psychologist, 47,* 1102–1114.

Rappaport, J. (1985). The power of empowerment language. *Social Policy, 16,* 15–21.

Rogers, E. M. (1995). *Diffusion of innovations* (4th ed.). New York: Free Press.

Rossi, P. H., & Freeman, H. E. (1993). *Evaluation: A systematic approach* (5th ed.). Newbury Park, CA: Sage.

Runes, D. D. (Ed.). (1983). *Dictionary of philosophy.* Savage, MA: Littlefield, Adams Quality Paperbacks.

School-to-Work Opportunities Act of 1994. (1994). Pub. L. No. 103-239, 108 Stat. 568. [On-line]. Retrieved February 5, 1998 from the World Wide Web: http://www.stw.ed.gov/factsht/act.htm

Seidman, E. (1987). Toward a framework for primary prevention research. In J. A. Steinberg & M. M. Silverman (Eds.), *Preventing mental disorder. A research perspective.* (DHHS Publication No. ADM 87-1492, pp. 2–19). Washington, DC: U.S. Government Printing Office.

Seidman, E. (1988). Back to the future, community psychology: Unfolding a theory of social intervention. *American Journal of Community Psychology, 16,* 3–24.

Shadish, W. R., Jr., Cook, T. D., & Leviton, L. C. (1995). *Foundations of program evaluation: Theories of practice.* Newbury Park, CA: Sage.

Shields, P. M. (1994). Bringing schools and communities together in preparation for the 21st century: Implications for the current educational reform movement for family and community involvement policies. In R. J. Anson (Ed.), *Systemic reform–perspectives on personalizing education.* [On-line]. U.S. Department of Education, Office of Educational Research and Improvement. Retrieved December 7, 1998 from the World Wide Web: http://www.ed.gov/pubs/EdReformStudies/SysReforms

Sink, D. W. (1991). Transorganizational development in urban policy coalitions. *Human Relations, 14,* 1179–1195.

Sternberg, R. J., & Spear-Swerling, L. (1996). *Teaching for thinking.* Washington, DC: American Psychological Association.

Thagard, P. (1992). *Conceptual revolutions.* Princeton, NJ: Princeton University Press.

Charles T. Diebold is a PhD candidate in Community Psychology at the University of Missouri-Kansas City. His research interests include empowerment, program evaluation, psychometrics, multivariate statistics, community change, collaboration, complexity theory, and emergent philosophy.

Ginny Miller is Director of Integrated Services at The Learning Exchange responsible for operations of the BE[2]:School-To-Career Partnership. Her research interests are teacher growth and change and the impact of workplace experiences on teacher beliefs about curriculum and pedagogy.

Leah K. Gensheimer, PhD, is Associate Professor of Psychology and Director of the Community Psychology, PhD Program at the University of Missouri-Kansas City. Her research interests include community psychology, program evaluation, prevention and health promotion, and children and youth issues.

Elaine Mondschein is Executive Vice President of The Learning Exchange responsible for the development, implementation and evaluation of Learning Exchange programming. Her background includes research and teaching in the psychology of learning, program design and evaluation.

Harold Ohmart, PhD, directs evaluation efforts for the BE^2: School-To-Career Partnership at The Learning Exchange. He has a doctorate in curriculum and instruction and researches efficacy principles applied in education.

For Product Safety Concerns and Information please contact our EU
representative GPSR@taylorandfrancis.com
Taylor & Francis Verlag GmbH, Kaufingerstraße 24, 80331 München, Germany